A BLACK BOY AT ETON

About the Author

Dillibe Onyeama is a Nigerian author and publishing executive, who founded the publishing company Delta Publications (Nigeria) Limited. In 1969, he became the first Black person to finish their studies at Eton College, and went on to attend The Writers' School of Great Britain. He has published twenty-eight books – both fiction and non-fiction – covering a wide range of subjects, including biography, education and self-improvement. He lives and works in his native Enugu, in south-east Nigeria.

A BLACK BOY
AT ETON

Dillibe Onyeama

With a new introduction by
Bernardine Evaristo

PENGUIN BOOKS

PENGUIN BOOKS

UK | USA | Canada | Ireland | Australia
India | New Zealand | South Africa

Penguin Books is part of the Penguin Random House group of companies
whose addresses can be found at global.penguinrandomhouse.com.

First published as *Nigger at Eton* by Leslie Frewin Publishers Limited 1972
First published as *A Black Boy at Eton* with a new introduction by Penguin Books 2022

001

Text copyright © Dillibe Onyeama and Leslie Frewin, 1972
Introduction copyright © Bernardine Evaristo, 2022

The moral right of the copyright holders has been asserted

Set in 11.6/15pt Fournier MT Std
Typeset by Jouve (UK), Milton Keynes
Printed and bound in Great Britain by Clays Ltd, Elcograf S.p.A.

The authorized representative in the EEA is Penguin Random House Ireland,
Morrison Chambers, 32 Nassau Street, Dublin D02 YH68

A CIP catalogue record for this book is available from the British Library

ISBN: 978–0–241–99381–1

www.greenpenguin.co.uk

MIX
Paper from
responsible sources
FSC® C018179

Penguin Random House is committed to a
sustainable future for our business, our readers
and our planet. This book is made from Forest
Stewardship Council® certified paper.

To
Walter Davis
In Priam Memoriam

Contents

Publisher's Note

In this book are some expressions and depictions of prejudices that were commonplace at the time it was written. We are printing them in the book as they were originally published because to make changes would be the same as pretending these prejudices never existed, and that the author didn't experience them.

Introduction

I came across this electrifying memoir many years ago when I was researching forgotten literature about black Britain. Its original title, *Nigger at Eton**, was so provocative, I wondered why I'd never heard of it. I managed to locate a second-hand copy and discovered that the author, Dillibe Onyeama, a Nigerian, had been a pupil at Eton College in the sixties, and that almost as soon as he matriculated, he wrote about his experiences there. I started reading, and the story he had to tell was so gripping and shocking, it wouldn't let me go.

This is no ordinary memoir because Eton, arguably the world's most famous school, has embodied and emboldened Britain's class system for hundreds of years and spawned an astonishing number of prime ministers – twenty, including the two most recent males, David Cameron and Boris Johnson, a worrying contradiction to contemporary beliefs about class and social progress.

Into this establishment hothouse of 1,200 boys with its archaic traditions, rigid hierarchies and a culture of corporal punishment

---

* The editorial decision to change the title to *A Black Boy at Eton* was made because we wanted to make sure that there were no obstacles to people wanting to read and talk about this book.

whereby older boys are authorized to beat their juniors, arrives fourteen-year-old Onyeama, who becomes only the second black African to attend the school.

The son of a Nigerian supreme court justice, who was later appointed a judge of the International Court of Justice at The Hague, Onyeama is clearly the progeny of a powerful and prosperous man, although this makes absolutely no difference to how he is perceived and treated by his fellow pupils, who throw the full weight of anti-black racism at him throughout the four years he attends this ultra-elite boarding school. It's hard not to be horrified at what he endures or to be outraged on his behalf. The imaginations of his peers have been cultivated to see black people through the imperial prism of the racial phenotypes and stereotypes that were concocted to justify the transatlantic slave trade and the British Empire. Instead of attempting to engage with Africa's multifarious nations, cultures, languages and belief systems, they were conveniently written off as thick savages who nonetheless possessed impressive physical prowess. Within this context, Onyeama is never allowed to be just another boy at the school. When he doesn't perform well academically, it is to be expected, and when he succeeds at sport, it's taken for granted. Further, when his grades are good, he is singled out for special attention because his classmates believe he has overcome the intellectual limitations of being black or, in some instances, rumours spread that he has been marked leniently to compensate for it.

Interestingly, for those who argue that, because racism was rampant in the sixties when Onyeama was at the school, this isn't exactly news, it's worth noting that the author, who arrived in Britain from Nigeria at the age of eight, did not suffer from the same level of abuse he encountered at Eton while at his previous British schools.

One of the book's greatest strengths is that, while he is clearly a sensitive boy who becomes attuned to all the nuances of racism he encounters, Onyeama is also a formidable fighter, literally and figuratively. Rather than submit to oppressive forces, he defends himself and thus manages to maintain his dignity, even though it often provokes more of the same.

Published in 1972, four years after he left the school in 1968, this is a remarkably well-written memoir, especially by someone still maturing into adulthood. With events still fresh in his mind, the author has the fluent facility to bring them to life with drama, passion and energy. Somewhat sadly, however, without the benefit of hindsight and still very close to his material, he is also terribly tough on himself to the point where you want to take him aside and commend him on how he navigated such enormously challenging circumstances. Reading about his early experiences of familial dislocation while still in Nigeria at a young age before migrating alone to Britain, where he finds alienation and victimization, makes it easier for us to understand and empathize with his predicament.

One hopes that the persistent dehumanization of someone on account of their ethnicity within the British education system would be unthinkable today. Onyeama was not treated kindly by many of the boys, and while superficial friendships were formed, the 'vicious little Caesars', as he describes them, come across as a mob of feral bullies who put him through hell. *They* are the savages who will one day become Old Etonians, with all the status, privileges and networks this bestows. One wonders how many of these future 'masters of the universe' will have gone forth into the nation and infected it with their insular sense of class and racial superiority from influential positions in politics, the judiciary, media, finance, the sciences, academia, arts, banking, business and the armed forces.

When *Nigger at Eton* was first published, Eton's then headmaster, Michael McCrum, banned Onyeama from ever visiting the school again. Rather like the Catholic Church, its violations behind closed doors should not be permitted to tarnish the reputation of such an august institution. After publication the book soon disappeared without trace, although Onyeama reissued it in Nigeria after he returned home. The author of many books since, he also helped to set up Delta Publications (Nigeria), before eventually becoming its current CEO.

Fifty years later, British journalist and writer Musa Okwonga, of Ugandan parentage, published his own memoir about attending Eton in the nineties, *One of Them* (2021). By then, the overt racism of earlier eras had gone underground and it was only many years after he'd left that Okwonga learnt about the racial aspersions cast behind his back by his classmates. During the Black Lives Matter protests of 2020, when many institutions were challenged on the murky pasts they'd rather remained hidden, the current headmaster of Eton apologized to Onyeama for the abuse he'd encountered half a century before. Okwonga reflects that the bigger issue for debate, about which Eton has always remained silent, is that 'the history of the British Empire is intimately connected with the history of Eton'.

Yet the past is never dead when we are alive to resurrect, interrogate and reinterpret it, and we must always strive to hold to account those who cloak themselves in moral rectitude and glory while refusing to acknowledge the source of their wealth, prestige and power. Onyeama's story about landing in the hostile environment of Eton College is a personal one, but the questions it raises have much wider repercussions.

Bernardine Evaristo
August 2021

Author's Note

Everything I say in this book is true. The characters mentioned are real, but many of the names have been changed to avoid possible embarrassment to persons living and relatives of those who are dead. Any similarity in such names is unintentional and coincidental.

Before I started writing, three writers in turn spent months attempting to re-write an earlier version I had committed to paper. After fifteen months, their attempts met with scant success.

For a number of reasons, all three concluded that the material my manuscript contained, along with further material supplied by me at their request, was insufficient to make a full-length book.

During those fifteen frustrating months I was undergoing extensive training at an established writers' school in London: thus, I hope, I acquired some writing experience to tackle the book myself, in my own words, finally submitting it – much to the irritation of my publishers – in long-hand.

I wish to express my sincere gratitude to the 'ghosts' for the time and unproductive effort they devoted to my original manuscript. But for the encouragement and advice of one in particular (a good friend who wishes to remain anonymous), I would never have had the inclination, patience or endurance to re-write it.

Dillibe Onyeama

Chapter One
Arrival

Eton! A renowned community destined to govern my life for nearly four years, and probably influence it for the rest of my days. Nearly 5ft 10in. tall and rather plump, I was going to be dumped down at great expense among more than 1,200 boys – just one of two blacks among them. Every detail of my first day is etched with sharp, bold strokes into my memory. It was ominously grey, cold and miserable, and fitted my mood perfectly. It was the 19th January 1965, two weeks after my fourteenth birthday. I was driven there, vibrating, from Glympton, a small and very quiet Oxfordshire village, set in a low area and surrounded by a river and hilly fields, with a population of 130. I had spent my Christmas holidays there with my guardian, the Reverend Arthur Cox, an ugly and fierce-looking man with a snub nose who, oddly enough, had no double chin accompanying his 6ft 5in. and seventeen stones. He was at the wheel of his Consul Cortina with his calm, little wife Nora by his side; ill with despair, I sprawled in the back seat, dressed in a dark suit. We had left the vicarage sometime between 3 and 4 p.m.: so soon because all new boys were requested to be at Eton by six; Etonians didn't have to return till ten.

Eton was fifty-two miles away and, due to Mr Cox's being a fast driver, we were able to lap up the miles in an hour and a quarter. And, my God, that journey was like a nightmare, and I wanted to disappear. Almost throughout I was submerged in a sea of deep thought, almost hypnotized. I was totally unaware of the world outside; I was not consciously aware of the fact that all the windows were closed and smoke from the Reverend Cox's pipe filled the car. Usually I detested this, for it caused me to feel ghastly and car sick. It was no doubt due to smoking that Mr Cox suffered from an asthmatic cough, which didn't seem to discourage him. Neither his coughing nor his conversation with his wife affected my thinking. I was only distracted when Mrs Cox occasionally turned to ask if I was all right, told me not to worry, and that I would soon get used to Eton. She had to call me two or three times before I was aware she was talking to me; and I must say her motherly voice cheered me slightly, but, more than anything, filled me with a mixture of nostalgia and fear to the extent that I felt like breaking down into choking sobs. I was worried to the scalp! I was filled with a sense of utter hopelessness and desolation.

My thoughts were on ragging. I was expecting to be a butt for ragging for some boys and a strange enigma to others; the former especially I feared. Now and again during my six years in England, I had heard blood-chilling stories of bullying at public schools, and found them most off-putting. One in particular had been the film *Tom Brown's Schooldays*, which was shown when I was about ten at my prep school. The ragging Tom Brown went through at Rugby, the agony and hardship he suffered, alarmed me and indeed my schoolmates. The only relief for us was that

4

the film was 'just imaginary', but I got to understand after seeing it that every new boy experienced ragging at public school. I never looked forward to Eton, especially during the years that followed when I was told by people, like masters and even my own father, that I certainly would be ragged.

As I sat in the speeding car, I wasn't merely worried that I would be bullied, but more so than any other boy – more roughly and pitilessly because I was black. I was led to believe this because of what I was told at a small Crammer I attended for only one term, and whence I passed my Common Entrance into Eton. It was after lunch one horrible, dreary day, a few days before term ended. I was packing my trunk in my dormitory when lanky Charlie Nichols entered. He was a quiet twelve-year-old, fair with a protruding backside and a permanent blush on his face. We said hello and he went to get a book by his bed. He stood there silently for some seconds, as I packed, then cleared his throat and with a sincere and somewhat timid voice told me I wouldn't be popular at Eton. I faced him inquisitively and asked why. He replied that he had a brother there, several years older than he was, who had told him that Tokunbo Akintola, the other African at Eton, was unpopular because of his colour. I received this with concealed shock and surprise. It was completely new to me and it had never occurred to me to think about it. My only reply to Nichols was that it was unfortunate, and he left. For a few minutes I stood there in my dark flannels and sweater gazing through the window and thinking worriedly. I was encouraged to believe him, for we had always got on well, and I saw no reason why he should be making it up just to get me worried. He'd said it in a way which seemed that he felt it a good idea to tell me, so I'd know what to expect and perhaps be prepared for it. I, in return, felt it was tactless of him to tell me, and I was put off considerably. I was totally ignorant of what racialism was all about, and I couldn't understand why colour should make Tokunbo Akintola unpopular.

However, until I was in my guardian's car, I had forgotten all about it. As I reflected on the matter and remembered certain events during those holidays at the vicarage, it seemed that the situation at Eton was going to be grim!

The vicarage was a neighbourly looking house with leaves and flowers growing on its walls. It was supposed to be over 800 years old in parts, though it didn't look it – from inside or out. The only signs of old age were the very creaky floorboards and staircases. It was a spacious, two-storey house comfortably resting in a largish garden. Contained in the garden was part of a river called the Glime. Only the splashing of this river down by the small falls disturbed the silent nights.

The vicarage was a holiday home for (mostly public school) students, of both sexes, whose parents worked abroad. Mine were in Nigeria, where my father was a Supreme Court judge in Lagos. The house could take twenty students, though only about half that number usually came; we slept in dormitories. The Reverend Cox was not guardian to any of the others: only to myself and my brother who, three years my junior, was at a prep school in Hampshire. Mr Cox became our guardian through his brother, who worked in Nigeria and was my father's great friend. For over two years I had holidayed mostly at the vicarage. Normally I'd found it an enjoyable holiday home, but that Christmas before Eton, it seemed like hell! It was a hurtful and bitter Christmas. Some of the students, only the boys, started victimizing me. For no reason whatever they molested and taunted me continually. In the billiard room, television room, during breakfast when Reverend and Mrs Cox were not present, they aggravated me, laughing and making unpleasant jokes – none of which was racial. Being highly sensitive, I was always deeply bruised and irritated. Usually I remained quiet. Sometimes I swore at them, only to be sworn at back. Even in front of the girls they continued, but no sympathy came from the girls. Some of the jokes were so comic that they tickled even my quiet brother, who was usually uninterested and didn't wish to be involved.

I kept out of doors as much as possible to avoid the taunts. I rambled across the fields, and more often than before took the bus to Woodstock, a small town three miles off; and sometimes to Oxford, twelve miles away. I spent the day visiting shops and going to the cinema. Most of the time I was fishing in the river, a great hobby of mine at which I was quite successful. I often had to fish outside the garden, for my tormentors came with their taunts, threw stones in the water, and ran away laughing.

Five boys tormented me – all in their late teens. They had come to the vicarage sometimes in previous holidays. They had started on me several days after the holidays began and went on almost every day for over a fortnight. I could do nothing except live with it. On a few occasions I quietly went into the lavatory to cry, vowing never to come there again. It seemed to me that they only made my life a misery out of sheer spite and sudden dislike for me. They had never done it before, and I couldn't understand what lay behind it all. I often seriously thought of complaining to Mr Cox or his wife, but felt it would sound too childish. If the boys had accompanied their taunts with physical molestation, it would have been reasonable enough to complain, but as it happened it was just mouthwork.

I was totally ignorant that Mr Cox, and no doubt his wife, was well aware of the taunts. He drew me into his study after lunch one day with an expression of great thoughtfulness on his face. Hardly had we entered the large room than he spoke.

'Now then! . . . You're not getting on well with the other students, are you?'

I shook my head and said no, I wasn't. He asked me why and I gave him my reasons in one sentence.

'And you should be thanking God, Charles.' He waited for the shock waves to subside. 'You should be glad. Do you know why they're teasing you?'

I shook my head and looked at the carpet. I was beginning to feel vaguely guilty by now. I was sure that somehow I was to blame. He went on. 'They're preparing you for Eton, Charles, preparing you . . . They know you hate being teased, and they *know* you're going to get a bad time of teasing at Eton; they know it from experience at their public schools, and they're preparing you for it. If you want to get on at Eton, you've got to stand up to teasing. So don't think it's because they don't like you. All right?'

A choking rage almost suffocated me. I wanted to break every precious thing in that grey man's study. I would not believe he could be serious, but he was; I could not believe that he expected me to believe the story, but he did. Nodding bleakly, I left the study.

He was Oxford-educated, and vicar of the small church in Glympton. He had three grown-up daughters, one married and the others working and coming to stay only at weekends. I didn't feel a great fondness for him. He was very quick tempered and as fierce as he looked. Perhaps it was because he was an officer in the Second World War, then, for a time, a policeman and finally a parson. He was a strict disciplinarian and often used to chastise, shout at and threaten the students for offences like laziness, untidiness, contradicting him and arguing – the last two of which he deplored most. I was perhaps the greatest offender for the first two crimes, and was beaten several times, deservedly enough, though I hated discipline. He used a slipper or a thin cane, both of which were very painful, especially with his size behind the strokes.

Mrs Cox, on the other hand, was kind and quiet as a mouse. It was during meals as we dished into her excellent cooking that full-scale rows between Mr Cox and one or more of the students, always boys, ensued. Occasionally I was one of them for reasons like not making my bed properly, fishing in my shoes, instead of gumboots, and so bringing mud into the house. All arguments always ended with, 'Shut up, boy! Get on with your meal and don't argue!' But offsetting his bad temper, he had a great sense of humour and was quite amusing at times. We all got used to him and accepted him for what he was.

His lecture to me about the taunts did two things: eased off my bitterness against my tormentors and made me sincerely wish that

I was not going to Eton. The few remaining weeks of the holidays were really terrible. Worrying about ragging was my main obstacle, accompanied by the continuing taunts, which didn't bother me so much now that I knew the reason for them; but I still hated them. They seemed to lessen, too. I thought that perhaps my guardian had told the boys to go easier. I wondered, too, if he could by any chance have told them to do it in the first place, but, as I never discussed the matter with anyone, I never found out. If he didn't, he certainly must have agreed with the idea . . .

As I cast my mind back with a terrible focus, in the car, it seemed that the situation at Eton was going to be as bad as *Tom Brown's Schooldays* – my colour being the reason. There was no possibility of the frightening journey being a fantasy. I was even tempted to wish that my blackness could be just a dream, and I was white instead. I begged that what Charlie Nichols had told me at my Crammer about prejudice at Eton was incorrect.

Soon we rounded a bend and slowed down. This instantly brought me out of my thoughts. I sat bolt upright, now very much awake, and there was a signpost staring down at me: ETON. The blood sang in my head. My heart started on a jazz rhythm. Nerves vibrating, senses fully alert, I looked at everything my eyes could take in. My first impression was that it was a perfectly ordinary place, despite big buildings and narrow lanes here and there. Nothing seemed to explain the reason for the celebrated name it had earned. It certainly did not look in the least hostile or ominous. That was the main thing I was trying to detect. And only a few people passed, mostly grown-ups, no tough-looking teenagers to add sparks to the fear gripping my heart.

A few minutes later the car swung into a narrow lane before turning into the drive of Waynflete House, where there were a few other cars. We had arrived. My stomach was knotted with fear as we struggled from the car and I looked up at the big, four-storey house. It looked old and a bit unwelcoming. I carried my luggage to the front door, where we were met by my housemaster and his wife, both of whom I had, in fact, met a year before, when the Headmaster of my prep school brought me to be interviewed.

My housemaster was one of the school's chaplains, and taught Classics. Long-faced, he was as old and as tall as the Reverend Cox with a permanently bowed head, which almost concealed his clerical collar. He had the rather disconcerting habit of not looking you straight in the eye when he spoke, and my first reaction was that he might turn out to be a rather unsympathetic character. His wife, however, seemed very cheerful, and the one counterbalanced the other.

After I had formally shaken them both by the hand, my housemaster, David Wild, took me to see my room, which was on the top floor of the house. Only at Eton did every boy have his own room in which to work, sleep and entertain his friends: it was his haven to decorate virtually as he pleased. After only a few terms, it became as familiar as the walls of a prison cell. It was a largish room, rather bigger than I had expected, with one small window looking towards Windsor Castle, about a mile away across green fields. The room was shiny and old, and the smell of furniture polish assailed my nostrils. The furniture was spartan-utility with a bootbox, an ottoman, a burry (a desk used for all purposes with a removable top on it that was the bookcase), mirror, table and of course a bed, which folded neatly on end against the wall; during the day it was concealed by a curtain. There was also a fireplace and a bucket of coal beside it, because boys were 'privileged' to make their own fires in the evening for warmth. I found it a very impressive room on first sight.

The first person I met there was Mrs Mac, the boys' maid for my landing. She was unpacking my trunk, which had been sent on in advance. Stout, white-haired and old, she seemed a kindly enough person. After being introduced to her, I was taken by my housemaster to his sitting-room, where my guardian and his wife were with the parents of four other new boys. For about an hour we drank tea, ate cakes and biscuits and rather stiffly tried to make conversation among ourselves. I was heartened that the other new boys seemed amiable.

I took my guardian and his wife to see my room. They spent half an hour there, praising it, saying how lucky I was, and that I wasn't to worry, I'd soon settle down. They had said this about twenty times that day but didn't seem aware of it. Then they left. I went downstairs with them to say goodbye, and from the hall I watched the car drive out to the road and disappear. My throat went dry and I swallowed what felt like a chunk of piglead. My vertebrae turned into ice cubes! A surging wave of apprehension – terror – engulfed me in a cold panic. I had never known anguish so intense. I was terribly *alone* and felt I knew the meaning of the word fully. I blinked away hot tears welling up. Reverend and Mrs Cox weren't my parents, not even very close to me: but I knew them and now they were gone.

*

The rooms of the other new boys were on the same floor as mine, two of them on either side. After my guardian left, I went upstairs and stopped at one of their rooms, and entered. All of them were congregated there and we chatted amicably for some time. I admitted my fear of being unpopular at the school owing to my colour, and the ragging I might suffer as a result. However, I didn't tell them the reasons for my fear. When they doubted strongly what I said and classified it as nonsense, I was slightly happier – only slightly. After all they were new boys, too, so how did they know? . . .

Supper was at eight, and we ate with the dame of the house in the large boys' dining-room: it contained two long tables, both already laid for breakfast the next day. The dame was a very pretty woman with white hair. Aged about forty, she spoke with a Scottish accent and appeared rather charming and pleasant. She later showed us round the house. A dame at Eton used to be the equivalent of a housemaster many years ago, but today is equivalent of a matron-cum-housekeeper. She administers all the catering in the house, handles the staff problems and generally looks after the welfare of the fifty or so boys under her care. She was addressed by the boys as 'Ma'am'. Before my dame showed us round, we were all taken by my housemaster to the School Office, where we signed our names in the New Boys' Book, to become Etonians officially. School Office was the administrative centre of the school and was about a quarter of a mile from my house.

At about half-past ten that evening, as I lay wearily in my narrow bed listening to the voices and quick footsteps of the Etonians who had now returned from holidays, I was visited by the House

Captain. I was to discover that he was to be really the most important person in my early life at the school. It was he who meted out punishment, designated for whom we would be fags, and whom all the lower school boys feared most. Simon Rawlence was a big, handsome fellow with long, curly hair. He came in with a cheerful grin on his face. For ten minutes he rather stiffly asked me about Nigeria, then reverted to Eton. 'I hope you won't be worried by the large number of boys here. I mean, there won't be any bullying or anything like that, so have no fear.' I need not describe how relieved I was to hear that, for that was what I had almost killed myself worrying about.

'The only thing you need to worry about,' he went on, 'is the colour test; but that's a long way off yet. Well . . . in the morning a boy will come up and show you how to put on the uniform and tie, it's a bit complicated. Okay, I'll see you in breakfast tomorrow, then.'

An exchange of goodnights and he left. I lay pensively for some time wondering what the Dickens the colour test constituted. I mean, I knew what colour I was, and I was tempted to wonder if some fiendish inquisition might have been dreamed up for me. I was to find out.

Dawn came and I was awake to greet it. With a knock on my door Mrs Mac entered, bearing a large jug of hot water which she poured into my washbowl. Breakfast was at eight, so I had half an hour to get into my strange uniform. Mrs Mac gossiped for a few minutes, impressing on me how lucky I was to be at Eton, and how positive she was that I would enjoy its great privileges, traditions and way of life.

Then, for the first time, I struggled into my striped trousers and tail-coat. As I watched my fighting figure in the mirror, I couldn't understand why such garments were used as a school uniform; I didn't exactly favour it. In the years to come, it was to prove a great embarrassment to me in the streets of Eton and Windsor. Fortunately the top hat had been abolished.

As the House Captain told me, a member of the house who had been at Eton for only one term came in to show me how to tie the unique, white bow-tie and fix the stiff collar. The tie was, in effect, a narrow strip of linen, which was fixed to the collar stud, tied in a bow and tucked under the collar. It took me some time to perfect the art of tying it without making it dirty.

The boy then took me downstairs, and with my heart in my mouth, I walked into the dining-room for breakfast. *My first Eton breakfast.* A sea of moving white jaws became gapingly still as I entered. Almost complete silence momentarily fell and every head turned to look at me. My eyes must have rolled, my nostrils must have flared and I know I gave a small whine of alarm. How could I tell in the silence if the looks were hostile or just curious? Either way it was a nerve-racking experience. The meal was much the same as at any other school, I imagine, with porridge, hard bacon and fried bread. I put all this down my throat without realizing it, and even now I can hardly bring myself to think about it. I spoke only when spoken to, and that was by the dame, and only dared look up a few times at new arrivals who went to help themselves at the serving table.

The boys could only serve themselves at breakfast and supper, going out when they finished and leaving their plates in a trolley.

At lunch they were served by Italian waiters, as that was the only meal housemasters attended with the boys. Everybody had to stand silently in their places, except the House Captain, who entered with the housemaster and the dame together. On reaching his place he would say a two-word grace and everybody could sit down. He sat at the senior end of the senior table, and the dame, who attended all meals and dished out the food at the serving table, sat at the junior end of the junior table.

After breakfast, the other new boys and myself were summoned to the housemaster's study which was actually in the boys' side of the house. The rest of his living quarters adjoined ours and were called 'the private side'. He explained where our classrooms were (called division rooms at Eton), and told us the text books we would require and need to buy from Alden and Blackwell, one of the school stationers.

There were no lessons on the first day of term: the time was spent getting orders for the necessary text books, all boys seeing which masters they were to be taught by and which division rooms they were going to have to go to. This meant a great deal to Etonians, because the school is a large place and if you had one lesson on one side of the school and the next on the other, it would probably mean running part of the way to be there on time. Also, of course, some masters were known to be more lenient and sympathetic than others: if on the first day, for example, you found that your French master was a terrible fellow, you were stuck with him for the whole term.

Being my first term, I was oblivious to this and spent most of the day lolling around the old buildings, trying to get over the newness and strangeness of it all. Most of them were old and brown, built for another age, and neatly laid in green gardens not far from the river Thames. I clearly remember the very noisy jets banking lazily over Windsor every few minutes after take-off from London Airport, eight miles away.

Surprisingly the day passed without my facing any major affront, which I had thought inevitable. I was pleasantly surprised to notice that I received few stares in the streets, and this I subsequently thought was because I was mistaken for Akintola, the other African at the school. I did in fact meet him that day, late in the afternoon in an Eton short cut called Judy's passage. He was in a hurry and we only exchanged a few words of greeting. A normal-looking African of just below medium size and wearing glasses, he was, in fact, younger than I, but entered the school two terms before. He certainly didn't look like someone who had been suffering a lot from bad treatment.

Only one customary event occurred that day: after lunch the whole of my house assembled noisily inside the big house library, containing many bookshelves, to inform the House Captain whom they were 'messing' with.

I learnt that one of the privileges at Eton was that boys could have tea in their own rooms, with no more than six friends. Such a group was known as a 'mess', and for your first term the House Captain arranged new boys into groups of his choosing, since no one had had time to get to know anyone well after just one day.

To start with I thought this a fabulous privilege and liked it a great deal. But in due course my views were to change. I messed with two boys, Charles Coaker and Henry Lawrence, in the former's room which was next to mine. They were both cheerful and talkative, Coaker especially, a fair, lanky boy with a mouse-like face, and a habit of burping at tea. Lawrence, wearing glasses, was naïve-looking and a bit scruffy and tousle-haired, and was apt to daydream as he chewed. We got on great to start with, and our first tea was a tasty one with sardines and hot baked beans on buttered toast, bread, biscuits and cakes, all bought by Coaker and eaten before a blazing fire. We agreed to take turns to buy food when we became short. But for the time being, his 'sock' cupboard was very full. (Sock meant food, sweets, drinks or small snacks – anything. When, in tuck shops, a boy asked another to sock him, he meant treat him to something and when a boy was socking, he was eating something.)

Tea lasted forty-five minutes. On non-half days, the boys' maids cleared away for boys on their landings – we had to go to divisions; on half-days we had to clear our plates away and leave them at the boys' maids' kitchens.

The second morning was cold and foggy. I went to my first division together with two of the new boys in my house. We carried our books under our arms. A crowd of boys was standing noisily outside the doors of the division rooms, which were in a building called Montague James Schools on the South side of Eton, nearest to the Thames. They were awaiting the arrival of the masters. And now I come to think of it, I don't know why they were outside the division rooms on that occasion, because they always waited for masters inside. However, immediately I entered I became a spectacle, and those who had not spotted me had their attention drawn to me. The noise started to subside to almost total silence and, for several moments, I was faced with stares, blank stares. I felt horrible. The stares were not hostile, not friendly, just stares. Noncommittal, dead eyes, like animals', and directed at me. Clearing my throat, I started to speak to the two boys I'd come with. Murmurs and giggles started, and for the first time I felt nervous. The noise started again after everybody had taken a good look, and several started talking to me with others listening.

'Will you do a war dance to celebrate your entry into Eton?' one boy sarcastically enquired. Together with giggles from some, he was told to shut up by others, and my confidence was momentarily restored. Gradually the tension eased and most of the boys had the decency and sensitivity to hide their grinning faces, and I pretended not to notice.

The master at last arrived. There were about twenty boys in that division, and we sat through a boring forty-five-minute lesson on the Roman Republic, after which I went to my second division, which was in Alington Schools, a good five-minute walk away, which was all right since we had ten minutes between each division. 'Chambers' followed that. This was the mid-morning break, lasting half an hour, when boys went to their houses to have cocoa and cakes. Many boys preferred to dash off to tuck shops and buy their own refreshments. Not knowing this I slowly made my way through the streets, littered with Etonians, to my house. The word Chambers could also be used for the time and place it took place. For masters it was held in the School Hall, which was on the upper half of Eton High Street towards the Slough Road. There, rather than scoff buns and drink cocoa, they listened to any announcements the Headmaster might make, and discussed current affairs.

We had six divisions that day. Eton's work programme was perhaps like any other public school: four divisions a day on Tuesday, Thursday and Saturday (which were the half-days) and the other two weekdays had two more after lunch. At least none of the masters struck me as being harsh or unpleasant. Apart from dressing as they liked, they wore white bow-ties. Theirs were fixed on special collars and were known as 'stick-ups', and worn also by House Captains and other privileged boys in the school.

I did nothing particularly interesting that second day, except to play a game of football with the juniors of my house on one of the numerous school pitches. That particular game tested how good we were for house or school teams, or both.

Apart from the 1,200 boys of the school, Eton itself was a lively town with a further 2,000 inhabitants, most of whom were, either in some minor or major way, connected with the school. It was quite a noisy town. The school was constantly molested by jet-liners' noise; they nearly always came over low. Angry masters in division rooms were often forced to stop teaching till the roaring engines slowly died in the distance. And to accompany the planes, traffic was usually quite busy and noisy on Eton High Street, motorcycles being worst of all, because Eton was situated between two large and fairly populous towns – Slough and Windsor, both a mile away. Only Windsor was officially on bound to boys.

The atmosphere of houses, too, was noisy when most of the boys were there: records coming full-blast from senior boys' rooms, slamming doors, running feet, yelling and 'mobbing', which meant indulging in horseplay. When one spoke of 'mobbing somebody up' it meant to tease or rough him.

After breakfast in a house various things happened. Boys, still looking half-asleep, hung around by the slab just outside the dining-room reading their newspapers – ordered the previous term; others took them to their rooms. Fags ran errands to other houses and performed their duty in their fag-masters' rooms. We had thirty minutes to be ready for Chapel, which lasted twenty minutes and was immediately followed by divisions. To fit in all the boys there were two chapels – College Chapel and Lower Chapel, the former being the bigger and more senior. Bells from College Chapel rang for five minutes, and everybody was to be in his place before they stopped ringing. After four divisions with Chambers in between, came the forty-five-minute lunch to which we all returned longingly and thankfully. Immediately after that came fagging duties again. Boys lined up quietly outside the housemaster's study to have their work books, or orders for work, signed, and to ask to go out with parents or suchlike. Upstairs, the dame attended in the medicine-room and heard all complaints of health. Not having so much respect for her, boys waited there very noisily and her voice was often heard from the small room threatening to send away particular noise-makers. She also signed orders for items like clothes and games equipment after treating the boys.

Twenty minutes after lunch the streets were littered with boys in football kit trotting off to playing fields for fixed games. Boys in tail-coats and in 'change' were also about. (Change was a voluntary free-time wear which was also used for sports like squash, fives and gymnastics: an ordinary jacket, a white shirt and grey flannel trousers.) We weren't allowed into Windsor in change. Boys who weren't taking any exercise were free, and did all sorts of things in and out of their houses – working in their rooms, mobbing there, going off to Windsor, tuck shops, etc. With the exception of 'Specialists', post 'O' level students on their 'A' level courses, everybody had to do five exercises a week (two strenuous and three non-strenuous) choosing any day for their free one. Strenuous games were fixed ones like football and rugger, and non-strenuous ones were squash, fives, etc.

Fixed games only took place on half-days and lovely hot baths followed them. At about that time, the lively boys' maids, having prepared boys' teas in small kitchens, noisily pushed trolleys bearing plates and pots to rooms. Then their kitchens would be full of boys hurriedly making toast, boiling eggs and tinned food; fags went to their fag-masters' rooms taking out the requirements from their sock cupboards, again making toast and boiling food for them before finally going to enjoy their own teas. Tea, incidentally, wasn't compulsory, and boys often socked instead in tuck shops.

Tea was at 4.15 p.m. and after that one had complete freedom again till 6.15 p.m., the time for lock-up. This was when the boys' entrance door was locked, and no boy should be outside his house without permission. At that time, all non-Specialists had to observe 'quiet hour' which constituted their staying in their rooms for one hour and preparing set work for the next day. This was, of course, the quietest moment of the day in the house. Until supper at eight, boys spent their time making a racket in friends' rooms and on the landings. Medicine-room followed supper, and fags tidied the messy rooms of their masters. They were allowed to play the latter's records as they fagged.

Five-minute prayers were at nine, which the dame did not attend. It was after supper and prayers, before the boys dispersed, that the housemaster informed us of important notices to be pinned on the house noticeboards, asked to see boys, and said anything else on his mind. The day was now ended. Fun from games, and hardship from work, were over. And once out of prayers we wearily, if nois-ily, mounted the stairs for our comfortable beds. Some boys waited first outside the housemaster's study to see him, and others, Special-ists only, who were members of any societies, left the house for an hour or more to attend meetings. Upstairs, boys fetched hot wash-ing water from the boys' maids' kitchens, while others went to bath at their fixed times. Members of the 'Library' and 'Debate' chatted and patrolled the landings for about thirty minutes, to see that nobody came out of his room for no good reason.

As members of the Library, they were the equivalent of house prefects. The name was used for their own sitting-room where they played records, discussed the lower boys (who, generally speaking, were boys under fifteen and especially those eligible for fagging) and generally behaved as they liked. (The House Cap-tain beat boys in the night there.) It was usually made up of the top six or seven boys in the house, and theirs was the divine right to fag boys to do their chores. The Debate was eight or so sub-prefects who assisted the Library in maintaining order in the house. They had no sitting-room, but could own record players, and were allowed the privilege of fagging boys for jobs outside the house. Once or twice a 'half', they held debates in the Library at 10.30 p.m. with all the Library members. The half was a term and three halves made one whole year.

Inside boys' rooms at night, however, non-Specialists were to have lights out by 9.45 p.m., and everybody by 10.30 p.m. Until those times boys read or finished off work for the next day or in advance. On most nights of the week the dame and housemaster paid visits at different times before lights out to ask how they were progressing.

That was a typical day at Eton. It took two weeks for me to gradually absorb the rhythm of the place. I had settled down by then and knew my way around most of the school, and, of course, had made friends. I was more or less mothered by everyone in my house and shown great kindness; I was being treated much more kindly than the other new boys, with whom I got on quite well. On many occasions, for instance, boys offered me bread at lunch, and held doors open for me as I passed. I got the impression that everybody had been instructed to give me special treatment, because I might be feeling strange and out of place in this unique establishment, due to my colour. Almost every night I was visited by a member of the Library and asked how I was getting on. I knew the other new boys were not being visited so often. I always said I was getting on fine, as indeed I was.

I had met with some racial abuse in various parts of the school, like division rooms, tuck shops and in the streets; and admittedly, I felt quite hurt. But when I compared this to those hurtful Christmas holidays at the vicarage, I was slightly cheered: the present abuse seemed trivial and nothing like as bad. I really started to feel optimistic. My edgy fantasies based on *Tom Brown's School-days* began to recede. It was even possible to fantasize about a day when, in the civilizing influence of Eton, my very blackness itself would disappear. I sincerely believed that my career at Eton would be an enjoyable one, and wrote to my father and guardian telling them so, adding that they were completely mistaken about the ragging they had warned me against. I was to discover, however, that I had spoke too soon and there were many occasions when I regretted those words – bitterly.

Chapter Two
My First Year

As I had been warned my first problem was to be the colour test. It took place on a Sunday evening, three weeks after my arrival, coinciding with the first day on which new boys were expected to start fagging, and my problems were just about to begin. For the colour test, each new boy was expected to know the geography of Eton and Windsor in detail, all the colours of the school caps and scarves and what they represented. There were twenty-five house caps alone, so it was no mean task. We also had to know the names and initials of all housemasters, and where their houses were.

The test was held in the Library, which was decorated completely with pictures of beautiful strip-girls, a few of whom were stark naked. The fire was blazing warmly as the Library members, sprawled importantly in settees and armchairs, fired questions at us. Some of the questions were very difficult and it was always the thing to throw in a few tricky and even funny ones. For example, '. . . where's the Headmaster's bush?' All the Library members were smiling mischievously at this question.

The boy frowned, racking his brains for the answer, then shook his head. 'Sorry I don't know that one.'

'Well you should have been told!' came the shouting reply. 'However we shan't count that question. It's between his legs!'

It was good to have some comedy on such a serious occasion, and we drowned the proceedings with laughter.

We all failed the first test and had a re-test the following Sunday, which again I failed, along with two others. And at about half-past ten that night, we were summoned to the Library, where all the members sat with vicious looks, flexing canes. We got a hot blowing up by the House Captain. He warned us that if we failed again when we were tested the next term, we would be soundly beaten. The sight of those canes caused a knotting in my stomach and a cold chill ran up my spine; I vowed later on that I would pass the next test at all costs, even though next term was far away yet. A beating was something I had firmly resolved to avoid before I came to the school.

I still had fagging to contend with, however, and it was, of course, detested by everyone except those senior enough to make use of the fags. Fags were summoned in a house by a long, drawn-out shout for a boy. This was a signal to drop whatever you were doing and run like a demon in the direction of the shout. The last to arrive was given the job. Since the duty could entail a trip as far as Windsor during the daylight hours, it was worth your accelerating as rapidly as possible. Anybody who stayed in his room and 'shirked' a boy-call was beaten. Only members of the Library could deliver boy-calls. The Debate could only go round to a fag's room and quietly give him a job to do. Each member of the Library, as I have already mentioned, had two or three personal fags who were responsible for tidying his room, putting out clean clothes, and making sure that all his creature comforts were at hand. Jobs done by fags incompetently were punishable by either a fine or a beating, the latter requiring the housemaster's permission.

There is nothing much to say about my first few days of fagging, except that, like the other boys, I hated it: most of all because we had to contend with it for four terms. I didn't, fortunately, arrive last for any boy-calls or show any incompetence. But it was only the beginning: the future would tell. It was March and getting milder, and the pain and loneliness of the first few days and nights were behind me.

On one such mild morning I entered a Classics division. No sooner was I inside the room than I was greeted with ape noises and racial names from every side.

'Here comes the big black bastard', shouted one boy, which immediately won him a good laugh. Quietly, with concealed pain and confusion, I asked what it was all about, but only succeeded in starting off another spate of ape noises. I sat down and quietly arranged my books on the desk, thanking my stars that my blushing was invisible. Next I was approached by a handsome, sleek-haired boy, whose father was a rich banker. He took pride in making remarks to me whenever he could, and seemed to thrive on laughter at other people's expense.

'Do you like this country?' he asked. His permanently blushing face held a taunting smile.

'Yeah, it's okay,' I replied rather cagily.

'Do you like the school uniform?'

'It's not all that bad.'

As we spoke there was almost total silence in the room, for everybody was listening, mischievous smiles on most faces.

'Don't you feel ashamed to wear it?' the boy continued.

'No, why should I?' I answered, wondering what was coming.

'Well,' he said, closing the trap, 'I thought that since all Africans usually wore nothing, wearing this would make you feel ashamed.'

A ripple of laughter went round the room, and I was just explaining, rather unnecessarily, that my people did not go around naked, when a boy in my house turned on him. He was joined by a few others, and the classroom was eventually divided between 'nigger lovers' and 'nigger haters'. Things might have got quite out of hand but for the belated arrival of the master at that moment. After the lesson, several of my tormentor's followers crowded round him as we dismissed, as if expecting me to take some sort of action at his remark outside the confines of the classroom where they would defend him. But nothing further happened on that occasion.

That incident is very vividly branded on my mind. It occurred a few weeks after my arrival: not long after I had started to become confident that my career at Eton would be an enjoyable one. What I had feared most about Eton had started. The incident bit deeply, and caused me much pain. I had the impression that it had obviously been arranged beforehand. Whether it was done to test my reaction or just for the sake of annoying me, I was not sure. It was wounding and unprovoked, and I firmly decided that this was my last attempt at playing the quiet black boy who did nothing. This

29

had been the most hurtful of the racial taunts I had so far experienced in a division room. It was usually ape noises and names, which were not, at least, made directly to my face. Most of the racial abuse I had experienced was in the streets and tuck shops – 'Filthy nigger!', 'Wog', 'Black bastard', 'Go back to the filth where you belong'. Things were not helped by my not knowing what one or two of the terms meant. To start with I found it all rather puzzling, later sad and annoying and finally embittering. Though I had expected to meet racial abuse at Eton, I used to wonder seriously why these things had to be said. What was so bad about being black-skinned that I should be abused for it? I recalled too that in my early days in Africa, there were many whites living there. Nobody ever abused them for being white, and they never abused us for being black.

Two reasons seemed to me the most likely for the racial abuse: my abusers were simply colour prejudiced, or they merely wanted to impress their friends. In retrospect I believe it was more of the latter, and they may not have been necessarily colour prejudiced. But they undoubtedly meant what they said: by picking me out, the sole black figure, they obviously meant to be discriminatory. I thought that racial abuse was sickening and outrageous! There was something about it which made it much more serious, wounding and loathsome than any other abuse: something which made it seem so different, a cut above the rest. What made it seem like this was the boys' usual reaction when I was abused: the serious expectant stares they used to deliver me; as if they knew that something of unrivalled vileness had been said and were expecting an explosive reaction from me.

Be that as it may, I resolved to start hitting back physically. And that was exactly what I did. More often than most I would resort to violence or at least threaten it. This proved to be a big mistake, and I thus quickly became extremely unpopular with a great number of boys. The immediate result of my strong-arm tactics was an even worse outbreak of quite deliberate, unprovoked and unjustified racial abuse. Rumour flew round that I could only get out of trouble by using physical strength, that I hated all forms of racial abuse and just a few simple jibes thrown at me would be good enough to start a punch-up. What effectively happened then was that many who had nothing better to do, except use foul language, simply taunted me in places where they knew I could not retaliate physically. It was possible to be sacked from Eton for starting a punch-up in the streets, where the world could see, so this became a favourite forum for boys to shout abuse. I then had the choice of either ignoring them, which I found difficult to do, or retaliating with words. Often I did this with phrases like, 'filthy white trash' or 'albino bastard', which only seemed to amuse them.

When it came to the punch though, it was usually on the arm. But on one occasion that, suitably, took place in the gymnasium, it was different. I had been watching an exciting boxing match (which we won) and afterwards was talking to a member of our team, Timothy Fearon. He was a fair boy of medium size, tough and cheerful. Clever and good at games, he was about my age but a year ahead in work. Unfortunately he lost a very close and spectacular fight. Amid the shouts of boys lolling around and the bangs and clangs of the ring being taken down in the main gym,

31

he and I chatted outside in the passage, which led to four other smaller gyms.

After a time, a rather motley collection of boys from one of my divisions came sidling over and made as if they wished to speak to me. Tim Fearon did not know them, so said goodbye and left. I would have liked to have followed, but it would have meant losing face when I knew that the front-runner of the little gang, a scruffy, gum-chewing loud-mouth with tously, dark hair, was sure to be looking for trouble of some sort. He asked a few harmless questions about Nigeria.

'Do you look like your mother?' he enquired, which for some reason I said no to, for I look very much like my mother. He went on. 'Do you live in a house?'

'Of course,' I replied logically. 'What else do you think I live in?'

'Well, you see, I was under the impression that all wogs lived in mud huts and trees and wore nothing. Do correct me if I'm wrong,' he said in sarcastic, self-congratulatory tones.

'Well you are wrong,' I stormed, 'so just try and get your facts right in future!'

'Oh sorry, I'm very sorry,' he replied with a total lack of sincerity, which almost caused his companions to laugh. 'A few years ago, I saw a film on Africa and the women had bones through their noses. Has your mother got a bone through her nose?'

That did it! His smirking friends and his grinning, self-satisfied face, like a cat that had just swallowed a canary, blinded me with anger and caused my temper to go completely. I swung a powerful right-hander at his chin and caught him right on the point. He dropped to the wooden floor like an inert sack and lay there crying. The happy faces of his friends distorted with shock, and next they were shouting at me with disapproval. The commotion soon brought boys from every corner of the gym. They appeared quite hostile on learning what had happened, and I quickly left. I felt sure afterwards that if I had stayed they would have attacked me, and there is no knowing what might have happened. Younger Etonians are great believers in safety in numbers and can be vicious little Caesars.

That incident took place around the middle of my first term, and one unusual thing about it was that I managed to fell my tormentor with one blow. I wasn't usually so lucky. Of course, the incident reached the ears of many in the school, and inevitably worsened my reputation for being a vicious character, and my popularity further declined.

By the end of the eleven-week Lent term (the shortest), my justified reputation for aggression was fully established throughout the school. And the ceaseless taunting I met in view of that was the greatest problem I had that term. It annoyed and worried me more than anything else. Similar incidents became very common in division rooms before the masters' arrival. Concealing my misery by cynical bitterness I struck out more savagely, until the matter became a vicious circle. The more unpopular I became, the more the taunting grew; the more I struck out, the more they jeered . . . But, I have to admit, they easily used to get the better of me. It was usually a situation of me versus half the division room, and sometimes nearly everybody; that is between seventeen to twenty-two boys. On several occasions, though, a few sympathetic characters shouted at my tormentors to leave me alone. But the latter always used adamantly to refuse, and strongly argue that I shouldn't take things to heart so much, and I shouldn't always resort to violence. Much as I would have liked to, I knew I couldn't really hurt any of my tormentors, for fear of the gravity of the injury and the trouble I would be in as a result. Very few boys attempted hitting me back, for two reasons, I felt: firstly, I was black; and I knew too well that they had this idea that the whites were no match for the blacks in strength. And secondly, at 5ft 10in., I found that I was the biggest boy in all my divisions. (I reached over six feet by the time I was fifteen, and 6ft 2½in. by the time I left Eton, and in every division I worked in I found that I was one of the biggest boys.)

Inside my house, too, I had established my unpopularity, mostly with the lower boys. But the abuse began there later than outside the house, and it took time for the boys to follow the example set for them. Also the abuse came from only one small group, a term ahead of me in work. Though nothing like as bad or as continual as outside, it was all just as wounding, and on a few occasions I did resort to violence in the passages. When I was abused in lunch and in boys' rooms, where I couldn't start a punch-up, I took offence, threatened my tormentors with violence or that I would complain to my housemaster. Having shown my feelings, most of the other lower boys showed me that I was not to their tastes by having nothing to do with me if they could help it. They never came into my room for a chat, and usually ignored me when I went to theirs, unless I spoke to them. This did not worry me much, as I was happy just to sit and enjoy their exchange of jokes and stories. This was my relationship, on the whole, with the boys my first term and that was how it continued throughout my first year, getting more and more unbearable. In the holidays I never had the courage to confess to my father and my guardian that they had been right, in fact I even denied that I was experiencing any form of teasing, lying to them that I had a great number of friends, and that I was finding the school really enjoyable in every respect.

And indeed there were, in the swinging life of the school, many enjoyable moments. The privileges and some of the popular traditions were merits of the school. For a boy in his first year, life was not as good as for others. For, as long as he remained a fag, he was pestered right, left and centre by the boy-calls, living under the predominant fear of the Library. He had to watch his footsteps: he knew the members of the Library were ruthless, that they adored beating and were always looking for a chance to get someone beaten. He also knew that as a fag he was in the best position to make blunders, so he had to be very competent. A few continually blundering fags in my house were beaten during my first year. But fortunately I was never beaten for fagging and having great fear for the self-important Library members, I went out of my way to fag as competently as possible. A few times I was fined for forgetting to collect milk from breakfast for the Library's tea. And these fines were usually only a shilling and never more than a half-crown. They were written in a small book kept inside a little tin box in the House Captain's room, and would be collected from the offender in his room after prayers once a week by a member of the Library.

The only good thing about fagging was that a boy's fag-master tipped him one pound at the end of term. I can't say how delighted I was when my House Captain told me after my first year that my fagging days were over. Like the other fags, I looked forward to the time when I would get the privilege to fag, little knowing that it was to be abolished in my house when I reached that position.

Thus the life of a first-year student differed from the others'; his eligibility for fagging made it tougher for him. But putting aside the fagging and racial problems, fate seemed to hold it that my first year was to be full of unfavourable events. The most serious by far was my failure in Trials my second term. These were the exams held at the end of each term at Eton, obviously to test whether boys had learnt anything during the term. If a boy failed on two consecutive occasions, he would have to leave, unless special permission for him to stay longer was given by the Headmaster, and then he would have to remain in the same divisions the following term and not move up. The pass mark was ridiculously low and if any boy failed, it showed he had made very little effort to do his work during the term. Nonetheless, I and several other boys failed, and the news came as a great shock to me. I was so sure that I had done well in general that I boasted ceaselessly to boys, saying this and how easy I had found the exam papers. I was so impatient to hear the results, which were read out in the school hall by the Lower master (the Headmaster's assistant who had authority over the 500 or so Lower boys), that I asked my housemaster when he came into my room the night before the results were announced. Standing in my dressing-gown and pyjamas I faced him, smiling respectfully.

'Yes!' he snarled in his deep voice, 'I do know that you haven't done *at all* well in your Trials!' He then angrily looked at me in silence. His murderous blue eyes seemed to smoulder with cold fire, and I couldn't look into them.

At this shock news, my heart gave a sickening lurch. My legs almost gave way, and for a few seconds the whole world seemed to go black.

'B—B—But—' My throat jammed.

'I don't think you bothered to revise at all, did you?' he went on after some seconds that seemed an eternity. I mildly protested that I had, but he persisted. 'No you didn't. It's all this fishing! You've done nothing but fish all term.'

'Di—Di—Did I get any papers back, sir?' I stuttered feebly.

'Yes, about five or six. And that Latin paper you did this morning you scored practically nothing on. And all because of this fishing. If you fail again next half, there'll be trouble.'

On saying this he left, leaving me to stand there in agony. I felt the utter hopelessness of the situation. I felt dazed. The sounds outside the open window suddenly sounded like rivers of doom pouring in with a gurgle and a rush. The whole room seemed to spin round with a roar of confusion and unreality, and I felt I would collapse if I didn't lie down at once. The light was soon off, and I was lying under the sheets, tears silently streaming. I was particularly ashamed of one thing: most boys entered the school at twelve or thirteen, and so I was a bit older than them to start with. I was the oldest boy by far in every division I worked in. In fact my own age group was a year ahead of me in work. In view of all this I felt it was a disgrace to fail Trials, so easy with such a low pass mark. It was true that I had fished a lot throughout the term. Fishing had always been my hobby and I fished in parts of the river Thames that were within the school boundaries. But my housemaster was wrong. I had revised. I had given a lot of time to revision. I just couldn't believe that I'd failed.

Naturally I did not look forward to 'reading over', late in the afternoon the next day, in the knowledge that I had failed. There were about 300 boys in my block that term, and School Hall sounded like a football stadium as we all waited for the arrival of the Lower master. He was a grey, double-chinned man of about six feet, well known for his beating power. Utter silence descended on his entry. He began reading out the names, beginning with those with distinctions in their results and working downwards, slowly to the bottom, where I knew my name would be read out.

'Failures!' he finally shouted, an expression of distaste coming to his face. 'In Alpha division there were none. In Beta division . . . Viscount Astor, Barclay, Lord Burgersh, The Hon. Mr Keyes, Onyeama, Palmer, Smith-Maxwell and Yorke-Long.'

The others among the failures were not easily picked out in the sea of tail-coats and identical striped trousers. But there was no difficulty in locating where I was standing. All heads turned and I felt very nervous and confused.

There was not much reaction among the boys at my failure, no doubt because everybody was looking forward to the next day, the holidays. Several did come and express their sympathy. There was one particular conversation which summed things up. Lanky Charlie Nichols and two of his friends met me some time after the reading was over, halfway down the High Street. And amid the noise of traffic and other things, we had a brief conversation. He was a scruffy, but friendly, fellow, and a sociable ruffian who in years to come became one of the school's tallest boys at 6ft 7in.

'Hard luck, Ony,' he said with deep solemnity, 'it must be bloody difficult for you to pass these exams.'

'Why must it be difficult for me?' I questioned glumly.

'Well, because you're an African, you see,' he explained, as if revealing a universal truth. 'And it's not really your fault.'

'Oh fuck off, you bloody white trash,' was my spontaneous reply and I left them, no doubt in dumb incomprehension as to the reason for my offensive reply.

I meant what I said. He thought he was being polite, but did not realize that the implication of his words was abusive: Africans could not expect to be brainy, after all they had just climbed down from the trees! I continually met with similar implications throughout my time at Eton.

However, I was greatly worried about failing Trials again next term. When my housemaster said there'd be trouble if I failed, I took it to mean that I would be sacked. One cold and cloudy afternoon the next term I had a chance to discuss this. It was on the way back from football on the famous playing fields of Eton, which were as usual littered with footballers. I was walking back with Tim Fearon, the boxer, whom we met earlier. A friend of his was present. I asked Fearon what he thought would happen if I failed again. He was reassuring, saying he didn't think I'd be made to leave.

'Don't worry,' he said. 'Besides they wouldn't dare chuck you out.' His voice was sincere and his words cheered me. 'You'd most likely get beaten by the Lower man. But you definitely wouldn't get chucked out.'

'Why not?' I asked, frowning inquisitively.

'You just wouldn't be.'

'But why should they chuck other boys out and not me,' I persisted.

'Well . . .'

'Because you're a nigger,' interrupted his friend, hoping for a laugh. But Fearon immediately let fly at him, shouting abuse and telling me to ignore him, which I did; but the point was made.

'What difference does it make about me being chucked out, just because I'm black,' I asked.

'Because if you were thrown out of the school, it would get in the papers and most probably a political row would result,' Fearon explained. 'You see, everybody nowadays is incredibly race conscious and it would all boil down to racial prejudice. That is what the school would be frightened of.'

The point had never occurred to me at all. But in the event I did not fail a second time, so the school was not faced with that problem.

Another unfavourable event during my first year was the one that I had firmly resolved to avoid at all costs: a caning by the Captain of the house. This also took place in the latter half of my second term. The news that I was to be beaten caused great excitement in the house and sparked off a new spate of racial abuse. As the house made its way up the stairs to bed after prayers I kept feeling pats on my back from the more sadistic of the lower boys. 'You shouldn't worry,' they said gloatingly. 'The cane should have no effect on you because Africans have such bloody thick skins, don't they?'

I miserably went to my room and ignored them. It showed their ignorance of Africans but rubbed salt into the wound.

I was summoned to the Library by one of its members at about eleven o'clock in the night. I had tried to pretend to be asleep when he came in but it made no difference. I was shaken awake and told to put on my dressing-gown, and then go and stand outside the Library door. The clammy fingers of fear gripped my body as I slowly went down the stairs. Every idea of getting out of it came to my head but was abandoned. After a wait of five minutes outside the door I was called in.

'Boy!'

Every member of the Library was present, sitting in a circle round the room with grim expressions on their faces.

'I suppose you know why you are here,' snapped Simon Rawlence, the House Captain. It was his last term at the school. He was flexing a long swishy cane destined to be laid across my backside.

'No,' I replied, genuinely not knowing the exact reason for my summons.

'You don't? Well, I'll tell you. You're here because you've been bloody rude to the Italian waiters. Whenever you finish breakfast and supper, you go out, then go back again a few minutes later and order them to get you more food as if it was their duty to get you more. Have you no respect for your elders?'

'Y–Yes,' I replied feebly.

'Well, why don't you show it then? There's no excuse, Onyeama. And I'm afraid that for your rudeness I'm going to have to beat you. Take off your dressing-gown.' I did so slowly and placed it on the floor. 'Now bend over that chair. No, on second thoughts, you're too big, so touch your toes.'

'I–I–I can't.'

'Well try then.'

I shut my eyes tightly as he brought the cane swishing down across my bottom. The strokes were slow, and after the fourth stroke I leapt up screaming – justifiably I thought afterwards. Due to its great flexibility, the cane had coiled right round my backside and caught me in the balls. As I nursed the agonizing pain, Rawlence shouted. 'Get down! Get down, only two more.' The last two strokes were not quite as painful as the others and I got up.

'Thank you, Onyeama,' he said, as was traditional, 'now go to your room.'

I picked up my dressing-gown and as I was about to go out of the door, I turned and grinned rudely at the other members of the Library who had silently witnessed my beating. Immediately I was recalled by one of them who shouted: 'Take that bloody grin off your face! . . . Stand outside the door again!'

Once more I was summoned inside.

'Onyeama,' said Rawlence calmly, 'for laughing behind my back I'm going to give you two more. Take off your—'

'But I wasn't laughing at—'

'Yes you were, and don't bloody lie!' shouted the other members together.

'You've got to learn to show us respect, Onyeama,' said Rawlence. 'Now bend down again.'

I hardly felt the extra two strokes because I was so numb from the previous six, but I resolved never to be beaten again (and I never was). There was considerable amusement among the other members of the house the next morning when they heard about the extra two strokes, and several times that day I kept hearing from lower boys, 'I told you you wouldn't feel it because of your skin.' I didn't tell them about my howls of pain, or indeed what had caused them. I deemed it judicious to say nothing more. I felt I had deserved it and I am sure that there were no undertones of racial prejudice. I did not think this then and I'm sure of it now. Other boys were beaten for far more trivial offences than that.

I had come pretty close to a beating earlier that term, by failing the colour test again for the third time. The other two new boys who had failed with me the previous term passed, leaving me to face the consequences alone. But to my surprise and relief I was not beaten as Rawlence had promised us. Instead I was summoned to the Library in the night and given another severe blowing up.

'Next week there'll be another colour test *just* for you,' Rawlence finally said harshly. 'Just for bloody Onyeama! And if you fail it, my God, you really will be over that chair and beaten bloody hard!'

Thanks to luck, I did not fail again. I had absolutely no idea as to why I was let off a beating, but I strongly felt that somehow my colour was my saviour. I discussed it the following evening in a room with several boys, and they agreed on one point: if it had been an ordinary Etonian, he would certainly have been beaten. But being black and the only one in the house, the Library might have thought my housemaster would not allow it, as it would have carried the undertones of racial prejudice if *only* I was beaten. Perhaps they had asked him and he had refused for that reason, who knows? That sounded to me the most likely reason, and I thanked the gods for painting me black.

So, apart from the colour abuse and fagging, those were some of the most worrying events my first year, and it seemed that being black was important in that it had influence over them: the school would think twice before sacking me if I failed Trials twice; the Library thought twice about beating me for failing the colour test. I was always very aware of allowances made for me, and they were cropping up continually throughout my time at Eton. One might well think I should have felt more than proud and happy to be black because I got away with things the others did not; honoured perhaps, like a guest. In some cases, as with the two I have just mentioned, that was so, but with most affairs it was not. On analysing the reasons for the allowances, I found them distasteful and somewhat abusive: I was looked on as an inferior because of my race and colour – that was the truth of the matter. Not expected to be up to the standard of the white man.

My other greatest worry, my first year, was my academic progress. This was one of the best examples of where allowances were made for me. My progress, compared to the average boy's, was terrible. My usual place in the fortnightly orders for most subjects was between the last six. The majority of masters I was up to were doubtful if, at this rate, I would get the required five 'O' levels to remain in the school. I was getting up to thirteen 'rips' a term from them, and over half that number by the middle of term. A rip was a bad piece of work returned with a tear on top of it by the master. It was to be signed by a boy's housemaster and 'Classical tutor'. Briefly, the latter's job was to see to boys' progress till they finished 'O' levels; and also to hold discussions and readings with them twice a week. This was called 'Private Business' and was supposed to broaden the pupils' outlook. His pupils were from different blocks for work, and he grouped each block in sixes and saw them at different times.

I needn't explain that thirteen rips a term was appalling. The average boy got around five or six, and if he got them too frequently, he was put on 'white ticket'. This was a piece of paper given out by the Lower master and Headmaster for repeated bad work or severe offences in divisions. And while on it, a boy was not allowed to go out of Eton with his parents or relations, or even by himself, as a punishment. He could only come off white ticket when all the masters who taught him reported themselves satisfied with his progress or behaviour. This could be for any length of time from eight days. Any further complaints from his masters, and he would be beaten as well as put on white ticket again.

Except for a few of the boys who failed in Trials with me my second term, nobody else I knew was getting anything like as many rips as I was my first year. Many boys went on white ticket just for a few rips, and the other Trials failures were often on. But not once in my time at Eton was I put on, though my housemaster and Classical tutor often threatened me with it. I recall several occasions in divisions when, before the master's arrival while most of the boys noisily mobbed around, an unfortunate Dick or Harry would moan at his desk, showing a few sympathetic friends his white ticket. I would go over and take a look. 'Hard luck,' I would say, 'I've got twelve rips and I haven't been put on whiters yet.' They would all freeze with incredulity. 'Why the hell not?'

'Of course,' one would then say almost scornfully, 'they've got to make special allowances for you.'

'That's true,' the others would realize, somewhat glumly. 'So it's all right for you to talk.'

I never, as far as I can remember, made any reply to this, because there was just nothing to say. I believed it was the truth, and it made me feel very uncomfortable. Because I was an African, my brains were inferior to the white boys'. That's what the boys thought, and no doubt that's why I was let off white ticket. White ticket was given after a discussion and agreement in Chambers between a boy's tutors – housemaster and Classical tutor (a housemaster, incidentally, was referred to by boys as 'tutor' or 'my tutor'). My Classical tutor was a lean, baby-faced man in his early sixties with glasses; thin-haired and with a bushy moustache. He was very strict: far stricter than my somewhat passive housemaster. Among other things he deplored rips, and quite a few of his pupils went on white ticket just for about four rips, often the same pupils. It was the same story with my housemaster and the boys in my house. But I always got away with it. Obviously he and my Classical tutor agreed that I should be overlooked. I of course hated the idea of being put on white ticket, but more, hated the reasons for my exemption, and genuinely would have preferred the former. But I could do absolutely nothing about it. It is a natural thing in a school to find many students who are not bright. There were many of them at Eton, and I was one. As I will show, throughout my life, I had never been bright at school. But to the Etonians, it wasn't that I was naturally dim as a person, but that all Africans were naturally dim. The so-called primitive civilization of Africa, and the dark, funny ideas about the Africans with which their colonial ancestors had imbued their minds, made them believe that the Africans had little intelligence.

One more interesting example regarding all this happened when I was in the Headmaster's division my second term. He was teaching us Latin. One hardly ever saw the Headmaster, Anthony Chenevix-Trench. Middle-aged, he was a small, grey-haired man who spoke through his nose with a somewhat aristocratic accent, and had eyes of contrasting sizes. A man who was always inventing rules and abolishing traditions. He was very amusing in the division, enlivening our ears with jokes and stories, and telling us how he adored children. Though pleasant he might have been, he had occasion to be nasty to the Toms and Harrys who repeatedly did bad work which he had previously discussed in detail. I was often among several of the seventeen boys who scored between three to five marks out of twenty. He would angrily lecture the whole division and hand out rips. But he never gave me one. He used to just write something like, 'SHOCKING! Rewrite and pay more attention!' On one occasion he returned our work, a few shockers had had written on theirs, 'See me at 4.30 p.m.!' together with nasty adjectives and comments. I was one of the shockers with two out of twenty, but just had to rewrite the translation, while with that and a rip, the other boys were beaten. And outside the confines of the division room, the boys' reaction to my situation was the same old story. 'God! How bloody unfair! . . . Oh, of course, I suppose you're different!'

I could think of no other reason except my race that the Headmaster always overlooked me. And all I could do about it was feel bad and uncomfortable. But I must admit that I felt, on that particular occasion that he beat those boys, more than honoured to be black.

Countering my failure at work was my success at games. And for once I really did experience mad delight when my contemporaries felt it was because I was black. To them all Negroes were gifted at sports. My first term, I represented the school's Under-14½ football team, playing as a fullback. I was particularly useful for my kicking, which was described by the *Eton College Chronicle*, the school's weekly newspaper, as 'prodigious' and 'of great value'. Boys used to gasp with amazement at the length my kicks went and, as we walked back after the game, used to express their certainty that I was the school's most powerful kicker. Out of modesty I always doubted it, but I felt very much flattered; even more so when somebody would occasionally throw in a racial remark, like, 'You're lucky, you Africans are so much more powerful than us.'

That was the particular reason I enjoyed playing football and indeed the other games which I was good at, because I was an African and that would be the reason for all the praise for my prowess. I knew also it was quite nonsensical and nothing but sheer ignorance to attribute a chap's ability at games to his colour.

After being constantly racially abused, after having my short-comings at work attributed to me because I was black, and having come tacitly to accept that indeed I might be inferior, it was comforting and, indeed, a pleasure when my sporting ability was accredited to just that aspect of myself. It was good to know that the white man had some respect and fear for some 'characteristics' of blackness!

The game I really adored playing was Eton football, called 'The Field Game' – an Eton-invented game. It was rather unpopular because no other school played it and it was compulsory. It was played in the Michaelmas term, up till half-term, when football and rugger took over. It was a mixture of football and rugger, more the latter. Apart from the ball being dribbled as in football, everything else was roughly like rugger, with all the names in rugger substituted for Eton ones. There was a goal-keeper, but he wasn't allowed to use his hands to save. The game was played between houses, and occasionally against Old Etonians.

My first Michaelmas term, I found myself representing both my 'House Side' (the senior team in a house) and 'The Junior'. And in both games I played back and took all the long kicks. I only adored The Field Game because, during house matches, all the members of houses had to come and watch, and cheer and encourage their team. I looked forward to those house matches. Whether we won or lost, all I looked forward to was showing off my kicks, because I just lapped up the cheers and shouts of admiration and astonishment that resounded every time I booted a long one. I cannot describe the great feeling of pleasure that surged through me: my pride and arrogance.

At running I didn't do too badly, but I was no Jesse Owens. It appeared, however, that many boys thought I should have been. I remember during my first term, having watched me chase the ball in football and often beat or overtake my man to it, members of my team commented on my speed. They suggested that I should enter for the hundred yards competition, expressing their feeling that I might win the finals. I knew that it was merely out of admiration that they flattered me. To them running was renowned as the black man's game: he was the master of it. So my pursuing the ball seemed more spectacular, compared to a white boy. No compliments were given to boys whom I knew were just as fast as I was. When I told my admirers that I had already entered for the hundred yards competition, and that I could do it in 11.4 seconds, they were positive that I would win the finals, for the school junior record was that exact time.

Word travelled, and on the day the athletics events began, a much larger crowd than usual stood at the finishing end to watch my particular heat. It was a rather grey and depressing afternoon, but there was quite some excitement. My opponents were cursing their luck for being put against me. I was the first black Etonian to run at those tracks, and everybody was expecting something as dynamic as Negro Jesse Owens. As for me I was vibrating nervously, mad with myself for talking too much. I knew I couldn't achieve 11.4 seconds and never had. Because 12.00 seconds was my fastest time when I left prep school, I reckoned I must have improved, and saw fit to say any old impressive time. The starting pistol went, and very soon it was all over. There was much disappointment when I finished in 12.00 seconds, even though I won the heat. I, too, was shocked, for I hadn't improved at all. When boys crowded round me for an explanation, I panted that I never once trained for it and had felt very stiff, which in fact was the case. Disillusioned, and having cheered me all the way for nothing, more or less, they barraged me with advice and a few ape noises. I should come and train very often, because I could easily smash the school record. There was much anxiety in their voices. I felt it was out of respect for the black runner that they were so keen to see me run and break the school record. I was tempted to believe that an ordinary white boy who claimed 11.4 seconds would not have received such a large audience and so much attention. But the boys were to be disappointed, for I never practised or took running seriously; though I reached the finals, I never came first again.

Cricket was my most successful game, and in my second term I was promoted to the highest game for under-sixteens within three weeks of the beginning of term, after playing in four games. I managed to find a place in the school team. I was noted only for my fast bowling, and I became feared as a demon bowler apt to inflict injuries on the batsmen. I had in fact struck quite a number, giving them minor but agonizing bruises somewhere on the body: only a few had to discontinue the innings – the forgetful ones who didn't wear boxes to protect them. The batsmen's fear of my balls was partly due to the rumours that circulated that I was one of the fastest and most dangerous bowlers in the school. My blackness was the central reason for the fear and the rumours, I knew it. Because the boys had this set and vivid idea of the black man having dynamic strength – ape strength – much stronger than whites, my bowling seemed to them faster and more dangerous than any-body else's fast bowling. Truly, I was never aware of so much alarm given any other fast bowler. I felt that many of them were just as fast, even faster than I was. I really enjoyed it when, before games or nets practice, anxious boys would beg me not to bowl fast. 'I'm sorry, old chap, but I wouldn't be so good if I bowled slowly,' was my usual, arrogant reply. And I enjoyed even more the way they would stand at the wicket with unconcealed fear and uneasiness as I took my twenty-yard run. And I can say categor-ically that it was due to their fear that I got many boys out.

However, I did get respect for the value of my bowling, and in all the games in the different groups that I played in, I was the opening bowler and was usually taking the most wickets. My most successful moments were during house matches, in which I played for both the Junior and Senior team of my house. These took place about six times every summer, and I usually took an average of four wickets in both teams. I particularly remember the senior house matches, because members of the 'Eleven' played for their houses, and the Eleven was the school's top team, famous for its annual match against Harrow School at Lord's Cricket Ground, in London. Unluckily for us no member of the Eleven was in my house. However, several times members of the Eleven were among my wickets. In my first senior house match, which unfor-tunately we lost by one wicket, I took seven wickets: two of my victims were from the Eleven and two from the 'Twenty-Two' or second Eleven. This caused much attention in the school. For three days congratulations were showered on me, and, again, when my success was reported the following week in the *Eton*

College Chronicle. This reaction seemed to show that my success was something astounding and unique.

Perhaps seldom, if at all, had a fourteen-year-old boy playing his first term of cricket done so well in a senior house match. But I was black! All Negroes were gifted sportsmen! And in just about every senior house match which took place that term, masters, members of the Eleven and Twenty-Two would take a few minutes from their games and come and watch me bowling. Undoubtedly, I imagined they were thinking, a certain prospect for the Eleven. Many boys kept flattering me with that. I was encouraged to believe that a white boy in my shoes would not have caused so much stir and attention, but being the only black out of more than 500 white 'dry-bobs' I was very conspicuous. A dry-bob was the Eton name for a boy who played cricket; for rowing, which was more popular than cricket, the term was 'wet-bob'.

So that was how my first year at Eton fell out: black and aggressive, unpopular and racially tormented; academically dim and patronized. But as a sportsman, respected. This was to be the same throughout my time at Eton.

Chapter Three
My Background

The circumstances that brought me sailing from Nigeria to England, and on to Eton, started at my father's wish. Like the average African father, he desired that his children should have the best education he could possibly afford. My father was educated at Brasenose College, Oxford, where he got his law degree. During his five years in England, he of course came to hear of the famous public schools like Eton, Harrow and Winchester. When I was born he was a magistrate in Mid-Western Nigeria. He asked several of his English friends working there which English public school they thought would be the best to send me to, and the general suggestion seemed to be Eton as it was unique and world renowned. So my father took their suggestion and put me down for Eton at birth. Though he had only a university education in England, he had a lot of respect for British education, both because of its reputation as the best in the world and his personal experience of it. I might just add that putting down boys' names at birth became rare at Eton, and nowadays they are hardly put down below five or six. It is usually done three or four years before the lowest age of entry, which is twelve.

I spent the first eight years of my life in Nigeria, an

industrialized country, five times the size of the British Isles. Among its forty million people there were some 200 different tribes and languages, and it was still under colonial rule. I was born in a large, densely populated town called Enugu, the capital of, the then, Eastern Nigeria. I was the second in my family. My elder brother was the result of my father's cohabitation with an English woman. He was nine years older than I, and till the age of twenty was educated in Nigeria before going to university in England.

I did not always live with my parents. When I was about four they sent me to live with my uncle, for my father was often being posted to different parts of Nigeria, and thus the family was kept moving to and fro. My parents wanted me to have a permanent place to settle down and start going to school. They had, I recall vaguely, always had the utmost difficulty in getting me to attend nurseries. I used to rend the air with hysterical screams in adamant refusal to attend. On the few occasions that they managed to get me to go, I was always sent back home by the African teachers and classified as uncontrollable: I ceaselessly used to bawl for my mother, and refused to partake in any activity.

My memories of my early days start from when I lived with my uncle. He was a married lawyer around thirty, several years younger than my father. Short and stout with thin wire glasses, he, too, had been Oxford trained. He was a quick-tempered man who often shouted at his servants for incompetence. During my two years with him, his charming and rather reserved wife gave birth to a baby boy. He lived in a noisy suburb of Enugu, and the house he occupied belonged to my father. It was one of a number that my father owned in Nigeria – a big, one-storey building with six bedrooms and servants' quarters nearby. It was built next to the noisy road, with a balcony round the tin roof. My parents often stayed there when they came on leave.

On the whole I liked my uncle and aunt. They looked after me well enough and I was happy living with them. The only thing I deplored was that they were much more disciplinarian than my very patient parents, and did not spoil me so much. Because of that I showed them much more respect and fear. Due to my extremely rough and mischievous character, they had numerous occasions to beat me with canes and slaps, and I always went off screaming hysterically. This was habitually my way of reacting when grown-ups beat me. And many others did, for I was grossly cheeky and abusive. It was usually a heavy knuckle-punch on the head. That was the common way for grown-ups to deal with insolent children. Violence played a major role in the civilization of Nigeria. Africans are very sensitive people, and the average man is easily embarrassed by abusive language. Insults and other disputes were settled preferably with fists rather than words, and it was quite common to see two people exchanging blows in the streets, quite often women.

I lived the same sort of life as the typical African child. I was extremely sociable and mixed with all types of children of both sexes and all classes. My pals were mostly children who lived in the vicinity of my uncle's house. And our amusements included football in the streets, learning all the filthy language, directing it at passing women and running away, and many other pranks.

Visiting was something I did a lot. I was frequently visiting close relations, and during weekends and holidays, went to stay with those living outside Enugu. I recall that a few times I went to spend the holidays with my parents at the different places they moved to.

I was pretty popular with most of the folks I knew in Enugu, though I was a great pain in the neck. One particular reason for my popularity was because I had enormous ears for my age. People took great pleasure in taunting me because of them, much to my intense dislike. Teenagers and grown-ups would, now and then, pull them annoyingly. Fights between my playmates and myself were often started by their remarks about them. I can never forget that one of the prayers I used to say at church on Sundays was that my ears would shrivel a bit, so I could be left alone in peace and quiet. I used to honestly believe that my request would be granted.

My figure, too, added to the amusement and drew taunts, though not quite so much as my ears. Greedy, I had the appetite of a hog and was very pot-bellied indeed. Our common diet was rice, and our food generally consisted of a lot of proteins and starchy, spicy dishes, some of which we ate with our hands. There was no dish that I didn't like.

At Enugu I attended school. Mine was a mixed one a few miles from my uncle's home. It comprised three one-storey buildings joined together in a 'U'-shaped fashion on a large stony compound. It was set on a steep hill from where one could get a great view of the distant colourful landscape. It was a day school, ending at noon, and we took packed food for the mid-morning break. There were about 130 of us, aged between four and nine. I disliked the school, simply because I was extremely idle and hated working. But I got on well enough with most of the boys and girls I knew, and several of them were good pals who lived near my uncle's. As usual I was always fighting. On numerous occasions my red and white check shirt and khaki shorts uniform was torn to rags as a result, and I was reduced to tears as many times as I put other boys and girls in tears.

The teachers were all married women around thirty in age, and could speak English quite fluently. They taught English, arithmetic and art, and taught in Ibo, the chief of the five languages in Eastern Nigeria, and one of the three main ones in the country. English was, in fact, the official language in Nigeria, but most people spoke 'Pidgin' English, a form of language which would have been incomprehensible to the Englishman. Many people, however, could not understand a word of English. I first picked it up at the mixed school, and by the age of eight I could speak and read it easily, both Pidgin and the Queen's English. However, Ibo was the language I normally spoke.

The only form of sports at the mixed school were running and physical training on the stony compound. These were supervised by the teachers twice a week in the mid-morning. Though always sweating under the blistering sun, we never felt too hot, unlike the English in the summer. Owing to my laziness and fatness, it shouldn't surprise anyone that I was totally useless at these sports. And when I always ended up last, I was of course the centre of amusement among my mates and even the teachers, both of whom together ridiculed my fatness. I disliked these sports because I was bad at them and because they were compulsory, but at least I preferred them to school work.

That was one of my greatest troubles – too much play and too little work. All I looked forward to was the end of the school in the afternoon, so as to return home and play: we were not given homework. My academic progress was always disgraceful. We had end-of-term exams and I never once passed and every term I was around the bottom in my class. This plus my troublesome character continually earned me appalling reports, and kept me in my uncle's bad books. Despite setting me homework and beating me, nothing could improve me, and he just gave me up as a waste of time and money.

I was punished at that school more than anywhere else in Nigeria, and I had more fear for the teachers than for my uncle, and I feared them more than I liked them. Usually they were pleasant, but could be antagonized easily: and when that happened, they became quite formidable. And I, having a habit of antagonizing everybody, was frequently punished. For offences like cheating and lying, the usual punishment was a brutal knuckle-punch on the head. For offences like bullying, obscene language, swearing and making dirty passes and remarks to the girls, at all of which I was one of the worst offenders, the teachers used supple canes. And the way they beat would undoubtedly seem to the white man extreme and unnecessarily cruel, although trivial to the African. With unabated ferocity, a teacher would lash the offender all over the body, and the latter used to collapse to the ground screaming and writhing with dreadful hysteria, begging for mercy. But the teacher would bear down unmercifully upon him, and her strokes would be rapid and anything up to thirty. All the punishments were done in the classroom before the eyes of the fifteen or more students, who would all watch gloatingly with unconcealed pleasure. We adored watching the caning, after which the sobbing offender returned to his seat, rubbing his quaking, tortured body all over, and we felt no sympathy whatsoever for him. What's more he would be covered with bloody cuts and bruises.

Girls received exactly the same sort of punishment, for girls in Nigeria were on the whole treated on the same basis as boys. There was no 'ladies first' as in England: women had no priority. Many parents disciplined their children in such a way. It was, in fact, common really. And when such discipline was dished out by parents, relations, guardians and suchlike, the hands and feet were often used instead of canes. The disciplinarian, who was sometimes a man, sometimes a woman, was usually stopped from continuing his merciless onslaught on the helpless offender by adult friends, who used to run and hold him back with solemn pleas of mercy, saying it was enough now. Should friends fail to come quickly and hold back the enraged parent, the offender could be thumped senseless, as I saw happen on two separate occasions during my eight years in Nigeria. And when these clamorous beatings took place in rooms, cups and saucers were smashed into pieces on the ground, with others damaged and strewn around. The victim, after the agonizing ordeal, would be affectionately consoled by the grown-ups as he or she shook convulsively with bitter tears.

It was not only when the victims were children that they were punished in such a way, but right up till their late teens; for to the African, until you are twenty-one, you are still a small child. And even after those brutalities were meted out, it was common to see the victims later returning with apologetic gestures and submissiveness, and even siding with the chastisers as if their coercions were justified. And finally, there would be joviality between the two as if nothing had happened. Neither my uncle nor my parents ever beat me like that: it was either six or more strokes across the backside or slaps across the face.

My most memorable days were spent with my family in Lagos, the capital of Nigeria. By the time I was six, I had two more brothers, soon followed by a sister. My father was a judge at the High Court in Lagos, and a few years after I had gone to England, he was promoted to the Supreme Court. He was a broad, stocky man of medium height with a bushy moustache and close-cut hair. Though he maintained physical discipline for offences, he and my mother spoilt us and usually let us have our own way. Mine was a very happy family.

Lagos was a swinging city in Western Nigeria with 800,000 people, part mainland and part island linked by a bridge. The island and some parts of the mainland lay behind a facade of big, ultra-modern buildings sprawled alongside a festering and fly-blown slum that you could smell before you could see. Here lived the bulk of the people of Lagos, in a sleazy, shanty-town existence, scratching a living from the castoffs of the *élite*.

There were, however, some clean and respectable areas for foreigners and important Africans. One of them was Ikoyi, a large, quiet area where many white people lived. That was my home. It was a beautiful, picturesque place with enormous salt-water lagoons, and the white or green houses there looked similar to one another. Ours was a green, two-storey one set in a large, attractive compound. With a 'U'-shaped drive, it was alive with graceful gardens and hedges containing delicate, brilliantly coloured, tropical flowers. Numerous palm and fruit trees stood majestically against the African blue sky; we had a gardener to look after their welfare. Also a steward, cook and driver, and their home was the long one-storey servants' quarters in the compound, thirty yards away from our house.

My memories of my activities in Lagos are very vivid. The occasional family drives in our Jaguar during late afternoons and at weekends were really delightful. We often visited friends and relations in the heart of Lagos, watched my father play tennis at clubs, or went to enjoy the beauty of Victoria Beach on the Atlantic, where numerous white people swam and sunbathed on the golden sand.

I continued my wild and mischievous ways in Lagos and had a profusion of friends, again all of different classes. Having a bicycle, one of my favourite hobbies was riding around Ikoyi with those who also had bicycles, hunting and molesting girls and engaging in other pranks. We played football in one another's compounds, fought, fished and bathed in the lagoons. My father caned me a few times for the latter, the water being pretty unhealthy.

I also had a great attachment to my father's servants. They were youngish, and only the driver was married with a daughter three years my junior. During afternoons, I and my companions relished joining them and other servants of neighbouring houses to sit on a sandy piece of ground outside the back entrance to our house, nonchalantly watching all that passed on the moderately quiet road. As well as vehicles and people, it included black and white riders cantering past at intervals on the horses they were exercising for the Saturday races held in the city. It was enrapturing to listen to the loud gasps of the gloating servants at the shapely women who strolled past, and the remarks they usually passed – especially to white women, whom they seemed to consider more attractive than the black ones. They sometimes used to chase both black and white women, and occasionally succeeded in chatting both up. I don't remember them ever being more successful than that.

Lagos was the first place I made white friends. I had seen white people before, now and again, in the other parts of Nigeria that I had lived in, and naturally at my age was very curious as to why they were white – too young to know that there were countries where white people lived. In Lagos my father had an abundance of white friends, and at birthday parties in my family, a lot of our guests were whites. At home only a few white playmates were among my black friends, but at school there were many. I just accepted the fact that they were white and was hardly aware of their colour. But I might mention that I was very much aware of the great respect that Africans in general, particularly the lower and working classes, showed to white people. More respect than to top black people. It was as if the whites were superior to blacks. I was too young to wonder why this was so, and thought little of it. Many years later, however, when I came to England and learnt all about colonialism in Africa and the white man's power there, I looked back and realized why.

I was at a mixed multiracial day school in Ikoyi. The brother after me joined me there when he was four. My elder brother was at a public school in Eastern Nigeria, and the other two in the family were too young to attend school. My school was composed of a few elongated, one-storey buildings on a large grass enclosure with numerous palm trees overlooking a lagoon. There were about 200 students, aged between four and ten. The teachers were married English women, whom I found much more gentle and patient than those in Enugu: they never beat us, only scolded and made complaints to our parents. They found me the same pain in the neck as my earlier teachers had done, inattentive and very troublesome, and they complained frequently to my father, who, in turn, often beat me. But though my work progress was as appalling as in Enugu, my English improved much more under the English teachers.

There were no games or sports at the school. During the mid-morning break we had the swings and see-saws to amuse us. But I preferred to go around in a gang, bullying, ragging, taking others' packed food and fighting other gangs. I myself was frequently beaten up by gangs, which included a lot of white boys, and usually went off in tears. I was the habitual butt of many students over my too fat figure instead, now, of my ears; in fact I was rarely taunted about my big ears in Lagos. I vividly remember terrifying moments when I was running for my life with a gang in full pursuit screaming 'Fatty Bom-Bom!' and finally catching up and unmercifully bullying me.

So that was me in Nigeria: adoring eating and enjoying myself, at work a total failure, while at trouble-making an unmatchable expert. My two years in Lagos eventually passed, and the time came for me to take myself off to England. It had always been my father's intention to send me to England at around the age of eight and have a prep school education, since one couldn't take entrance exams from Nigeria for entry into a British public school. My only knowledge of England was that it was a white man's country and was very cold, and I wasn't at all enthusiastic to go there. My mild protests to my parents were always gently turned down, and it wasn't long before I was on a liner steaming across the Atlantic towards England, 3000 miles away. I left in mid-summer 1959, with my father and five-year-old brother, whom my father returned with after deciding he was too young to be left in England. My mother, who has never been to England, remained in Nigeria with the rest of the family. Though, of course, very sad at leaving my sweet home, the wonderful sun, my friends and my loved ones, I did not feel too miserable about it, as my father had made me believe that I would be back again soon.

We arrived in England after two luxurious weeks on the sea. I was immediately surprised but relieved that the weather was hot and not cold as I had been told back home. I was totally ignorant that there were different seasons in a year, and this was the summer season. The first place I had to gather my impressions was London, two hours by train from Liverpool. We were met at Euston station by a Nigerian diplomat, a great friend of my father's. As the chauffeur-driven car made its way through the streets, I was gripped with trance-like alarm as I stared into the hot, London afternoon; alarmed at the size and atmosphere of the place. The buildings were colossal and seemed uncomfortably huddled together as if to take up every available space. Much bigger than any building I had seen in Nigeria, they were depressingly grey and old, which gave London a rather unwelcoming atmosphere. My alarm was mixed with fascination at the size of the double-decker buses (which we didn't have in Nigeria), because I wondered, and still do, how the hell they didn't topple over when they turned. My first impression was that England was going to be grim and unlikeable.

We were in London for a week or so before my father had my brother and I fixed up with a school. While he stayed in a hotel, my brother and I stayed with the diplomat's family. His wife took both of us around London a couple of times in their chauffeured car. There was hardly anything that I found impressive about the place. It was nothing like as joyous, as lively or as spacious as Lagos: the enormous buildings had no big compounds, and there seemed to be no space for children to play. Somewhat forlorn, and sad at being away from home, I was for once quiet and inoffensive. I mostly sat glued to the television, which fascinated me greatly, since we hadn't yet got television in Nigeria. I recall that I was pleasantly surprised to see numerous black people, I had never dreamt that there would be many in England, and had expected to be quite uncommon.

The school that my father found for my brother and I was a mixed one in Hove, Sussex. With only about twenty students aged between four and twelve, it was merely a temporary place for us to start getting used to British ways until a prep school was found for me. We were there for several weeks, starting during the holidays and leaving a few weeks after the term began. The building was a semi-detached house, where only about eight of us were boarders.

I found Hove much younger and more cheerful-looking than London, and took a liking to it. Though I still missed the beautiful compounds in Nigeria, there was a back garden where we could amuse ourselves: the sea was only a few minutes away by foot, and I greatly enjoyed the numerous occasions we went there to swim and picnic during the holidays and the term. Of the school itself, I do have special memories. I remember how fed-up I used to get with the women teachers' obsession about manners. They used to fuss terribly about sitting up at meals: holding knives and forks this way and that way; ladies first; 'yes PLEASE'; 'no THANK YOU'. These were irrelevant and rare in Nigeria. But eventually I became used to the new customs and habits, and adapted myself to the *status quo*.

I remember that all hell was let loose in the school, especially after the term began. To start with, at work I was still as stupid and scatterbrained as ever, and the teachers used to get sick to the scalp with me. They used to become pretty sharp in an effort to get my attention during classes, but it was useless. Worst of all was my general behaviour. All the teachers, domestic staff and, above all, the pupils, really went out of their way to be as pleasant as they could to my brother and me. To many of the students we appeared strange, presumably because they hadn't seen or met blacks before. I never felt strange amongst them at all – having schooled with whites back home. However, I took everybody's kindness for granted and in return continued my wild and trouble-some ways. I virtually became the terror of the place! I was flagrantly rude and disobedient to the teachers and domestic staff, bullied the boys and girls and sent them off in tears. The teachers kept scolding me till they were at their wits' end. Never had they seen anything like it before! Time and time again I was reported to the Headmistress, a tall, sharp-looking woman in her middle-age. She was the only teacher that I feared. Apart from severe lectures, the punishments she gave me were missing supper, writing out lines, missing trips to the beach and smacks on my backside with her hand. Though she often threatened to cane me she never did. And much as I used to sulk after my punishments, I knew I deserved them. Every time my father visited us from London, she complained to him in private. His stern lectures when he took us for meals didn't change me.

Yes, I gave a very bad impression of myself at that school. My brother, however, was liked very much. Shy and extremely quiet, he was to everybody 'such a sweet darling'. In retrospect, I thank my bottom dollar that he was not like me; had he been, then the impression that we would have left of Africans in general would have been an appalling one (if that wasn't already the case, thanks to me). I think I quite enjoyed the school on the whole, though the teachers didn't like me and weren't, undoubtedly, sorry when I left.

My brother and I then stayed in London with a different Nigerian family than before, a couple with a small daughter. I was at their house for a few days only, during which time my father came to take me to be fitted with clothes for my new school. Then late one morning we went – leaving my brother behind. He was to return home with my father a week or two later.

My prep school, where I stayed five years, was in a small town called Crowborough, in Sussex: a town surrounded by country-side. I joined the school, named Grove Park, a week after it had opened for the Michaelmas term. It was found for my father by a great English friend of his, who once lived in Nigeria, and who was a personal friend of the Headmaster. Vaguely I remember that on my first day, much as I felt very lonely as I waved from the hall door at the taxi taking my father away, I was very far from tears: I was a boy of self-control and very seldom cried for any reasons other than physical pain. The very thought that I was being abandoned by my father alone in a strange, far-away country did not, honestly, worry me. In my slowly maturing mind, I knew that, being my father whom I trusted and loved, he would only choose what he knew would be best for me. So there was nothing to be bothered about, I thought.

About eighty-seven years old, Grove Park was a big building. At first sight, it seemed very peaceful and inviting. Situated in a moderately quiet area of Crowborough, it was enclosed by a vast wooded garden, and overlooked a big lawn used by the staff for tennis. Behind this lay the enormous games field. As a school, Grove Park was small with usually about forty-five boys a term, well under half of whom were day boys. There were five masters, the Headmaster included, and a woman teacher who took the fifth form, the lowest. The school was independent and was owned by the Headmaster, Mr Vivian Sharp. It was his home. He was an old, partially bald man, shortish and very fat. Because of his figure we nicknamed him 'barrel'. With a hoarse voice, he was a bit of a stammerer. His wife was a drooping, charming and smiling woman also on the fat side. They had a son in his early twenties who was at some university.

I was the first black boy to go to Grove Park, and I remember the great welcome I received from the whole teaching staff, matrons and the boys. For my first week it was like living in heaven: I was really heartened by the friendliness and 'guest' treatment, and I was very quick to settle down. Oddly enough, I was very peaceful for that week, though very talkative, lively and sociable, not my usual troublesome self. That was probably because I was interested in trying to get used to the new life that I was to follow. The friendliness of everybody virtually made me forget my country, and I had no loneliness at all. I was very impressed with my new experiences. I greatly enjoyed the organized football games, the long school walks across the country, and the cross-country runs. There was a big gym where we wrestled and fought, and also roller-skated which fascinated me but took a long time to master. I enjoyed the stories that the boys told in the six-bedded dormitory at night, and gradually came to understand British jokes and their meanings.

One of my immediate memories is how I loathed the cold climate. I remember that it took me a very long time to become used to it, and I received a great deal of sympathy from everybody. At the suggestion of Mr and Mrs Sharp and the two kindly matrons, I used to wear two sweaters over my shirt both when inside and outside the building. I used to be allowed to have hotwater bottles at night for a few weeks. The boys in my dormitory were never envious: in fact, they thought it only fair, as I had just come from a very hot climate.

Though I used to be often questioned about Nigeria by the boys, we accepted the fact that I was black and they were white, and I was never really conscious of the difference between us. But as time passed things were to change. I was caused to envy their colour, lose respect for my own people, and become ashamed of being black. There were two reasons for this. One was that as I became more and more used to the British way of life, things slowly started dawning in my mind. I began to notice and realize things. These 'things' were the discrepancies between African and British civilization. In my slowly growing mind I started to sense that the white man was superior and years ahead of my people when I compared certain aspects of their habits and civilization. I remembered certain parts of Eastern Nigeria, where it was nothing to see folk of both sexes, from the kids to the aged, pass in the streets almost naked, with utter abandon and obliviousness, and the vulgarity of their display whenever they sat down. And in addition the offensive manner in which they scratched their armpits, their breasts and their private parts in public. Then there was Lagos, where it was common to see people urinating in the street gutters. In Britain I noticed modesty, the finesse, and consciousness of the people to their families and environment. Britain clearly appeared much more advanced in all fields (and was generally much tidier). Yes, I began to remember Africa and now saw Britain, and I started to love it! My African environment went crashing, because I saw the Britain that was to be my future adventure – regardless of her ghastly climate.

The details of my life at Grove Park to some extent followed a familiar pattern with that in Nigeria and Hove. Firstly my work was always bad throughout my time at the school, and here lay my second reason for being ashamed of my colour. My fortnightly positions in my classes were usually near the bottom; during my first few years, I was frequently bottom. My schoolmates used to attribute the cause for my failure to my race. And I did not, to start with, receive this with distaste – as I was to do at Eton. On the contrary, I very much accepted their words as true. I genuinely believed that I was bad at work because I was an African. I remember the occasions in dormitories and classrooms when I used to moan miserably at my coming last in the fortnightly order. And boys would patronize me by saying, somewhat sympathetically, that I shouldn't worry: it wasn't my fault, Africans weren't as brainy or civilized as the English. I remember that occasionally I used to answer with a glum 'Yes I know'. I was too young to realize their ignorance and the abusive implication of their words, though they meant well and were also ignorant of what they were saying. The only resentment I used to have was the concealed one that I had to be black. In my naïvety, I started to think I was black by mistake; that somewhere, somehow, along in the machinery, there had been a terrific blunder and I turned out black. Which is to say that I thought only whites were supposed to be on earth.

Vaguely I recall that it was not until my last year or two that I started to become a bit more realistic about the whole matter. Although I knew, by then, that the whites were more advanced than my people, my attitude was that God planned us the way we were and still loved us, so I should therefore not be ashamed of myself. I remember that I started to show a more hostile reaction when the boys occasionally blamed my stupidity on my race. I had started to become aware of the abusive implication, and I used to take offence and defend my people. But I must admit that I always suffered from an inferiority complex.

There was another side to this question of colour. At games I had a great success. But naturally. Wasn't I an African? That was the idea held by my schoolmates. The games played at Grove Park were cricket, rugger and football. I managed to reach the top teams of each game by my third year, and was in due course awarded my colours for them. The details of my success at each game followed a similar pattern to that which I was to experience at Eton. At cricket I was a fast and feared bowler, and at football and rugger I was able to run fast, and also boot the ball. And because I was a black person doing all this, it seemed particularly spectacular and dynamic to my schoolmates, judging by their gasps of admiration. My excessive weight had, to a large extent, subsided in my early days at the school due to strenuous exercises, and the remnants of fatness didn't in any way inhibit my movements at play. At sports I also managed to prosper. On Sports Day, which we had every summer, with the attendance of parents, I always succeeded in winning the events I went in for: the hundred-yards sprint, quarter-mile, long jump and throwing the cricket ball. It was a pleasant surprise when, in my last summer, I broke the school record for the hundred yards and throwing the cricket ball, though not by very much. We never competed against other schools for sports.

Of course, I used to feel very proud and arrogant at my success. These feelings were also because I was black; for my school fellows used to say openly that we Africans were gifted at games and sports. To start with I used to believe it, I wanted to believe it, and I liked to believe it. But again, around the age of twelve, I started to realize that this was ignorance: you couldn't judge a person's sporting ability by the colour of his skin. All the same, it delighted me to know that my people were respected for something.

One can therefore see that my prep school experiences at work and games were mostly the same as those that occurred at Eton. But those academic and sporting experiences were the only ones of similarity with Eton. I never, for instance, experienced any abuse relating to my colour from anybody at Grove Park. I never heard the expressions wog, nig-nog or nigger, or any other prejudiced words. No boy ever expressed dislike for black people within my hearing. I suppose because we were all too young to know about colour prejudice, and that such a thing existed. I certainly had no notion.

I was violent at Grove Park, but only in as much as I was an ordinary prep school boy at odds with other prep school boys. My violence was confined to my first few years. During that time I was the same fighting, bullying, ruffian I used to be in Nigeria. I just fought for the thrills of it, and because it was part of my character. I used to torment boys, thump them and challenge them to a brawl in the gym. I remember that boys in my age group were always afraid to fight or hit me back. They actually used to say that Africans were stronger than Englishmen. So I was lucky to get off without ever being beaten up. In my last two years I became less playful, much more tranquil and more serious in my outlook than I had been.

I got on quite well at Grove Park and, on the whole, I enjoyed schooling there. I did have my enemies, and I also had a number of good friends whose company I was usually in. At many half-terms, they kindly invited me to spend the two-nights' break with their families. I liked most of the teachers who taught us. Among those who came and went were the nice ones, strict ones, unpleasant ones, odd ones, etc., and like the other boys, I came to accept them for what they were. I used to think that they also held the idea that my sporting ability and failure at work were both due to my colour, though they in no way hinted that they held that view.

With a ratio of one master to about seven boys, the educational standard at Grove Park was high, due to close, individual attention in the classes. Unfortunately, that could never improve me. My fault wasn't that I had difficulty in understanding the masters: I did not, since I had a fairly good mastery of the English language. I just wasn't brainy: furthermore I hated work and was frequently inattentive, for which I was often given lines by the masters and whacked by Mr Sharp, as were other boys. No allowances were ever made for me, I didn't hold back the rest of the boys in my classes by being dim, but usually I received more attention from the teachers than most boys in an effort to improve me. The same applied to other brainless boys.

Many of my memories of Grove Park are blurred and scattered, but there were certainly some happy days there. One thing I remember is that my younger brother joined the school in the Michaelmas term of 1962. He had come to England during the preceding holidays with my elder brother, who went to study medicine at Guy's Hospital, London University. It was comforting to have my younger brother in the school with me. Still his old quiet and shy self, he fitted in well and became quite happy. It was a year since I had seen him, or the rest of my family for that matter. I had gone home to Nigeria in the summer holidays of

1961, and also in summer 1962. My brother and I went together in 1963. For various reasons, my elder brother had been unable to go. Despite the fact that I had come to lose respect for Nigeria after comparing her with Britain, I always felt happy to return home again and see all my friends and loved ones once more. I usually spent the Christmas and Lent holidays with Nigerian friends of my family, and occasionally at English homes in Kent and Stafford to get more acquainted with English family ways. These were organized by Mr and Mrs Sharp at the request of my father. Not long after my brother came to England, the Reverend Cox was appointed our official guardian, and we started going to his vicarage home in Oxfordshire for our holidays.

It was at Grove Park that I first learnt about Eton. I used to read about it in the newspapers now and again, but really I knew very little about it: just that it was one of the best and most expensive schools in Britain, where boys wore tail-coats and top hats, and had their own rooms. I gathered all this from one of the matrons, whose job it was to come round and switch off the lights in the dormitories. Affectionate, she was a small, lively woman in her thirties with bunned hair. I vaguely recall that on a few occasions, during my earlier days at Grove Park, as the boys lay in their beds, she spoke about public schools. She used to speak very impressively of Eton, saying how lucky I was to be going there. She used to express her wish that she could afford to send her son there. He was about my age, and was also at Grove Park. I remember that, with a slight tone of envy, the boys would say to me 'lucky beggar!' I used to smirk and mock them all. Indeed I did consider myself very lucky. But then as time passed, occasionally in dormitories, I heard stories of ragging at public schools. Some boys used to tell of how their fathers had suffered from it, and I got the impression that it happened to every new boy. Subsequently I started to feel uneasy about Eton, and didn't fancy the idea of going there quite so much. My fears were worsened by the film *Tom Brown's Schooldays*, as I have said, and which I remember caused a number of boys to cry. We watched the film in the third-form, the largest in size in the school, where prayers were held every morning. (Grove Park enjoyed the privilege of being shown films from time to time by outside teams – usually documentaries and cartoons.) I recall that in my more senior years, four teenaged masters came temporarily on separate occasions. They had left their public schools not long before. In classrooms they sometimes held our interest by talking of public school. I remember that I retained my apprehension when they used to say that life was tough for newcomers, and there was some ragging.

Then I had a chance to see the very place that I didn't look forward to. In the summer of 1963, I went for an interview with my future housemaster at Eton. That day is rather vague in my mind; I remember at least that it was brilliant with sunshine. I was dressed in a grey school suit, and wearing 'longs' for this special occasion: shorts were our everyday wear. Mr Sharp drove me there around mid-morning, and his wife was beside him. I felt a sense of intrigue more than anything else: I just wanted to see what was so fantastic about Eton. I was also wondering if I would see anything to put me off – ragging perhaps? . . .

I remember that we had lunch in Windsor, after which Mr Sharp parked his car somewhere, and he and I walked down to

Eton without Mrs Sharp. We passed a good number of Etonians and I remember that my immediate thoughts were: are they the bully-types? . . . I didn't fancy the uniform. It seemed uncomfortable and just didn't look right for a school uniform. However, apart from that, everything else seemed perfectly ordinary. Certainly nothing was off-putting about the boys or the place. It seemed like somewhere I could get to like a lot.

My housemaster, I remember, seemed a kindly enough chap. The interview took place in his drawing-room, and in the presence of Mr Sharp. It went quite well. He and Mr Sharp discussed my work for a little while, and they decided that Lent 1964 would be about the right time for me to have a go at Common Entrance. Afterwards my housemaster took us to see some of the boys' rooms, and I remember that I thought it a fabulous privilege to be able to have your own room. Next we spent a rather boring hour looking round the school, and nothing of any importance that I can remember caught my interest. However, I recall that I was, on the whole, impressed by the general friendliness of Eton; it dispersed my thoughts of ragging for the time being and made me feel I would like to go there. I might just add that when I returned to Grove Park in the evening, I was bombarded with all sorts of questions about Eton by the boys and the teachers.

I took my Common Entrance in Lent 1964, and unfortunately failed. This didn't really come as a surprise to anybody. Though my work had improved greatly and I had occasionally reached pass-marks in old Common Entrance test papers, everybody doubted I would make it. I didn't actually hear them saying so, but I could feel it strongly – especially among the masters. They were obviously relying on a fluke – so was I actually. I was never confident at all. I knew, as I sat through the difficult papers, that I'd had it, but I was never bold enough to admit it to anybody. I always falsely expressed my feelings that I was doing okay so far. However, I accepted my failure without taking it too hard. I didn't know how much I failed by, because unlike other public schools Eton doesn't tell candidates their marks. It is either a pass or failure. However, in a roundabout way, my housemaster had told Mr Sharp that I failed dismally in all subjects except for divinity, which I just scraped through. Mr Sharp summoned me to his study one afternoon and gently told me. I shouldn't worry, he added, I would try again for Eton.

I might mention that I had a partner in failure in the school. Three of us had taken the examinations and only one passed. I did, I must confess, have a slight feeling of comfort at not being the only failure. Had I been, I would have felt terribly self-conscious, as I had sensed that the main reason everybody felt I was going to fail was because of my race. Many boys expressed their sympathy to me. Nobody, however, tried to suggest any cause for my failure.

And try again for Eton I did, but not from Grove Park. My father had come to England on a few months' leave from Nigeria around the time I failed my Common Entrance. He was, of course, disappointed about it, and when he came and took my brother and I to tea, he went on persistently that I should pull my socks up and start doing some serious work for a change. My elder brother had come with him. However, he spoke to Mr Sharp about what should be done with me, and went to see my housemaster at Eton. It was by and by agreed between them that I should leave Grove Park and go to a Crammer, and there do nothing but solid work in preparation for my second attempt at the exams.

I left Grove Park in the Summer term. So did everybody else actually: the school closed down for good, and the building was demolished a few years later. Unfortunately, Mr Sharp became ill in the latter half of the term. Doctors thought that he had been overworking and was too old to continue his headmastership. He was advised to give up and take a few weeks off. This he was prepared to do, but he was not keen to see his school continue under a new headmaster, and preferred to close it down.

He was about seventy; a smoker, and as a result suffered a bit from a throaty cough. He was on the strict side and was extremely particular about many things, such as tidiness, attention to work, punctuality and competence. He was quick to lose patience, and it was common to hear him bellowing at boys. Quite a disciplinarian, he often gave beatings with the back of a brush, and I often used to be on the receiving end for misbehaviour, inattention and bad work. Strict as he was, he often appeared extremely jovial; and when in a good mood, used to delight the boys during work with his great wit and sense of humour. He was also rather affectionate, and would often hug and pat you cheerfully. I think on the whole he was liked by most of the boys, though I myself, for no special reason, didn't particularly take to him. He treated me on the same level as he did the others, and never showed any different attitude. When it was known that he was to retire and Grove Park to close, it shook a lot of boys, and produced many tears. I remember that it was the most senior of his assistant masters who sorrowfully announced it to us just after breakfast one morning, in the dining-room. At the time Mr Sharp was away on the few weeks' break that the doctors had suggested. It was an extremely sad story, but we had to accept it as life.

The Crammer I went to after Grove Park was called Beke Place. Also in Sussex, though a long way from Grove Park, it was situated in the serene countryside near a small town called Billingshurst. It usually took about twenty boys a term, many of whom stayed there for up to a year before taking the Common Entrance. Its principal was a big, plump middle-aged man with glasses named Mr Thomas Flynn. He was an Old Harrovian, with a habit of clamping his jaw muscles. The Crammer was his home. He was married with two children, a daughter in her late teens and a fifteen-year-old son, who was schooling at Harrow. The main building of the Crammer overlooked a big pond and was accompanied by a smaller two-storey building, which contained a classroom and a dormitory. There were three teachers, and they lived out.

At Beke Place my progress improved greatly. This was not only because of the forceful teaching of the strict teachers, but also because for once in my life I had decided to have a really serious attitude to my work. The teachers nearly always had my full attention, and I was determined at all costs to pass the Common Entrance. I became a quiet character that term, and not as sociable as I used to be: I spent a great deal of my free time in voluntary work. My general percentage in marks had reached the seventies, and the teachers were more confident of my chances than before. When the exams came, I retained my confidence as I sat through the papers, and when, a few weeks later, I saw my name in Eton's list of passes, I was not, quite honestly, surprised. Out of some dozen candidates at the Crammer, I can remember only two who failed. There were four other boys taking the exams to Eton, and they all passed.

I was the only black boy at Beke Place, and I got on quite well with the others. I never met with any colour problems, but I remember that I picked up the expression 'nigger' there. I remember that in conversation, some boys occasionally used 'nigger' in reference to black people. I never dreamt that it was a racial name and generally used with contempt; I just reckoned it was a harmless slang word for a black man, and thought absolutely nothing of it. In retrospect, I remember that whenever the word was used, I was given glances by boys present as if to see how I might react. I was never aware of the significance of those glances. I only think now that everybody, including the users of the word, must have known that the word was bad and abusive. The users were obviously trying to be 'big.'

So that was Beke Place. Though not exactly the sort of place where one could expect to enjoy oneself, life was quite pleasant. The teachers, for instance, when outside the classrooms, were as agreeable and as good-humoured as you could possibly expect. The food was mouth-watering, and there were some great extra-curricular activities. Mr Flynn, now and again, took the Common Entrance candidates in his van to watch football and rugger matches, horse racing, and once to the cinema. He really was a jolly person whom everybody liked a lot and respected; especially the wit of his upperclass voice. But in the classroom, he was the most feared teacher. He kept a long wooden stick on the ledge of his blackboard. He would ask you to repeat something he had just explained if he suspected you weren't attending. If you failed, he would angrily beckon you to the board and deliver a hell of a whack across your backside with the stick. It was truly damned painful, that stick. I had it once, and succeeded never to have it again.

Eventually it was goodbye to all that. For the remaining few weeks of the term after the Common Entrance results arrived, I was enraptured by the thought that I had passed into *Eton* – the world's most famous school. I felt a sense of achievement, and I was greatly looking forward to going there, until Charlie Nichols came and drove all such pleasant thoughts out of my mind by saying I would be unpopular there because I was black.

Chapter Four
Eton and Etonians

There were few things more popular at Eton than getting about seven good storytellers into one room, particularly in the evening, and swapping jokes and anecdotes, apocryphal or otherwise about Eton and the things that happened there. I never put in any words myself, firstly because I feared that my unpopularity was enough to produce little interest or laughs, and secondly because I was a bad joker and storyteller. However, I played an active part when it came to mobbing, and always delighted the boys in the room by the way I mobbed.

Some of the things more popular than social chats in rooms included the school's traditions and privileges. Looking at the latter first, the most common were 'holidays', which must not be confused with the end-of-term vacations. A holiday was a complete day of freedom from work, with no lessons or organized games other than school matches. There were about four or five of these a term. Unless he was playing in any match, a boy was his own master and he had a variety of choices for spending his day. If he was the studious type, it was a marvellous opportunity to prepare or do work set in advance. If not, he could spend the day away from Eton, after getting his housemaster's permission two or three days before. Most boys were usually away from the school, and between mid-day and lock-up, by which time everybody should have returned to his house, Eton seemed much quieter and listless. Boys who owned bicycles went cycling, others went out with relations, or went home, or amused themselves in London, and some of the different societies within the school went on organized excursions somewhere in the country. Boys who stayed in the school continued life normally. Like everybody else, I very much looked forward to holidays and considered the affair to be a great tradition. Usually I remained at the school and messed around. The last thing I ever wanted to think of was work, and I never did any. Occasionally I got permission to go to the cinema in Slough and Windsor, and a few times visited London Airport to watch planes – a great hobby of mine.

Holidays were given for special days connected with the history of the school and the public, for example on 7th May (Ascension Day) and on 13th June, the Queen's Official Birthday. The most popular and exciting of these special days were 'Founder's Day' and the 'Fourth of June'. The former was every 6th December, when the whole school celebrated its founding by Henry VI in 1440. It was more than just a holiday. In every house after lock-up an atmosphere of ease and happiness gripped everybody. Impatient stomachs waited for 8 p.m., the time for the great feast. The dining-room was beautifully decorated with balloons and paperchains; lighted candles shone on the two tables instead of the main lights of the room. Just like Christmas. We ate heartily and ravenously, the food being roast turkey followed by Christmas pudding together with fruit, nuts and chocolates on the table.

On that particular occasion, the boys' maids helped the Italian waiters to serve us. Drinks of cider and beer were served by members of the Library, who were all dressed in dinner suits; only boys over sixteen could drink beer. Crackers were pulled and hats worn towards the end of the feast. Finally, great applause would follow a speech from the House Captain thanking the dame and all the staff for having prepared this mouth-watering meal. I might just add that a few masters and their wives were always guests at these feasts, and also the housemaster's wife.

And to conclude what had undoubtedly been a splendid day for everybody, a film show. Because it would be impossible to have all the twenty-five houses of the school seeing different films on the same night, three or four houses met together to watch the same film. The shows were held in boys' houses, School Hall and in the Science Lecture Theatre. And the projectors used belonged to the Film Society, masters and boys. The films usually shown to my house were comedies and were thoroughly enjoyed by everybody.

Equally popular as Founder's Day was the famous Fourth of June. This was held on that date, except when it fell on Sundays, and was to celebrate the birthday of George the Third, who was born in 1738: George the Third had always been kindly disposed to the school, and had an interest in what went on. From after chapel till the end of the day Eton was like a big festival. Houses flew their flags. Scores of police from Slough and Windsor came specially down to control the vast traffic of parents and relations coming to see their Toms and Harrys, and direct them to possible parking places. One of the football pitches near my house was packed with cars by mid-day. Sales of flowers and strawberries on the pavement along the High Street. Etonians proudly walked around with their families, some in their tails, and others wearing the abolished top hats. Entertainments were staged throughout the day and paintings displayed at the Art Schools. Cricket was played from late morning till late afternoon. The Eleven and the Twenty-Two played against Old Etonians. The former played on Agar's Plough, which was joined by Dutchman's Plough, as the two famous playing fields were known. Thousands watched the Eleven play, sitting lazily in deck-chairs, picnicking on the grass by their parked cars, and strolling around – in and out of the three white tents, where drinks and refreshments were served and books and magazines sold. Old Etonians were there, too, arrogant and happy, showing off their sexy girlfriends, and dressed in all sorts of fancy wear. The Twenty-Two did not have as many spectators as its big brother. It was played on Upper Club pitch, which was separated from Agar's Plough. I played in the Twenty-Two on my last Fourth of June, and succeeded in taking three wickets. My pride to have been playing is indescribable, for the reason that I was the only black and the first one to ever reach the Twenty-Two.

One of the most popular entertainments was the Procession of Boats. This was performed by the wet-bobs just after all the cricket finished. There was another identical performance at dusk before the fireworks display. About 4000 spectators watched from Fellow's Eyot, an enormous, beautifully kept garden overlooking the Thames. Boys with permission from the Provost could fish there, otherwise it was normally out of bounds to them; because it was the garden to the enormous old Cloisters building over-looking it – where the Headmaster, the Provost and Fellows lived, as well as senior masters. Local inhabitants also watched all the entertainments, from the opposite bank.

Eight boats took part in the procession, eight rowers per boat, all magnificently dressed in straw hats and blue eighteenth-century naval uniform. Each boat, thirty seconds after the other, started from a few hundred yards upstream and approached. When almost parallel to Fellow's Eyot, the rowers carefully and slowly stood up one by one, commanded by the cox, who was dressed like an admiral. This was where the excitement begun. Dangerously the boat swayed from side to side as each rower stood up with his oars. This sent a roar of excitement sweeping through the fascinated spectators. The suspense was overwhelming as suddenly the boat came within inches of overturning. Shrieks of exultation and delight swept through everybody when a boat finally did capsize, and great amusement would follow for quite some time as the occupants struggled in the freezing water. Though they could all swim, they were picked up by three tubs standing by and brought to Fellow's Eyot. The capsized boat would be pulled to the opposite bank by a tub.

In all the four summers I was at Eton, only about five times did boats capsize. But all the same it was all very entertaining, for very few boats avoided nerve-gripping tilts as the occupants stood still together for a few seconds, oars upright, before the cox ordered each in turn to sit down. Great applause went out to them as they triumphantly rowed off downstream.

It was nine o'clock by the time the one-hour procession

finished, so quite dark: just right for the fireworks display, which took place next and at the same place. It was the last performance of the day. The fireworks were operated from the opposite bank, and went on for an hour: an hour of flying, gorgeously dazzling colours exploding in the air with quiet fizzles or like detonating mortars, accompanied by shrieks of delight from the spectators, who were all ecstatic at the spectacle.

Finish! Everybody walked off in great spirits no doubt wishing it could last longer. But there was next year to look forward to. Soon the streets were strewn with cars of parents beginning their long ride home. Etonians made their way to their houses for their beds. Another great day was past.

No boy was compelled to be present for any of the entertainments on the Fourth of June, unless he was taking part in any of them. He was allowed to leave Eton for the whole day, so long as he was back in his house by 10 p.m. But so popular were the Procession of Boats and fireworks, that very few boys could dream of missing them. They would go out for meals alone or with their relations, missing everything that went on at Eton except the last procession and the fireworks. The last procession was more popular than the first one because, being in the evening, the creeping darkness made the whole atmosphere seem more exciting and the rowers more colourful in their uniform. Also, unlike in the afternoon, there was a feeling of great ease and gay abandon amongst the spectators. For these reasons I had always wanted my guardian and his wife to stay for the two evening performances and be impressed, but to my disappointment they never did, because Glympton was too far away and they didn't fancy driving back so late. They came to see me on my first two Fourth of June occasions, taking me out to lunch and tea, then going home after seeing the afternoon procession of boats – the only entertainment they ever watched, and that only on one occasion. They never came to see me at Eton again, for after spending the following Christmas holidays with them, I got a Nigerian guardian in London. The deathly silence of Glympton had become too boring for me. I wanted to start meeting more of my own people and see more of the outside world.

It was after that last summer they visited me that the Fourth of June's popularity collapsed horribly. The two evening entertainments were suddenly abolished; the fireworks because it was too expensive to arrange, and the last procession because, it was felt, one procession in the day was enough. Many more boys than before started spending the whole day away from the school, and didn't bother to turn up for the sole procession at 6.30 p.m. In place of fireworks, the term's school play was given one of its four performances, but its popularity couldn't be matched with that of the fireworks at all. I was able to get a part in one play called *Billy Budd*, a story of high adventure on the sea, taking place on an ancient sailing ship. I found it quite enjoyable, though my part only consisted of a few appearances as one of the sailors. Though I found the Fourth of June less good after the abolitions, I preferred to remain in the school rather than go out anywhere. Apart from watching the cricket matches and the procession of boats, I also adored weaving around on Agar's Plough, feeling arrogant; arrogant to be the only black in this renowned establishment (Akintola had left by then) and enjoying all the looks of curiosity from families. I really felt important, especially when a few boys I knew introduced me to their parents. I felt that this was partly because of my colour.

Perhaps one of the traditional events involving Eton best known to the world was the annual Eton and Harrow cricket match at Lord's. It lasted two days, and those two days were holidays. At around the same time, the wet-bobs would be having the regatta at Henley-on-Thames, some fifteen miles from Eton. And though rowing was more popular at Eton than cricket, Henley did not draw anything like as many spectators as Lord's. However I took no interest in rowing at all, and knew little about the rowing activities in the school.

Boys could go to Lord's with relations or in school coaches, but never alone. Most of the boys who went weren't so much interested in the match as being free, meeting people and behaving as they liked. And the general behaviour was not good. As well as trying to seduce girls, some boys drank alcohol (apparently it was allowed at Lord's) until they were drunk or were sick. A good example to illustrate the normal behaviour was in 1967 when I decided to go to Lord's for the first time. Sweating in the intense heat, I sat alone on a bench, dressed in a fawn tropical suit, to watch the game. But there was no peace. Nearby a gang of Etonians were mobbing together, and exchanging abuse with a party of Harrovians with shouts of 'Etonian bastards!' and 'Harrovian pigs!' A great deal of noise and obscene language, together with some stone throwing. Next, what looked like a fight was threatening. A big Harrovian stood up and with his mates eyed the Etonians challengingly. Then I was called by an Etonian I recognized, but hardly knew; a thin fellow in my block with long hair extending to his neck, dressed in a violently coloured silky shirt and bell-bottomed trousers. He wanted me to come and fight the big Harrovian; no sooner had he called my name than he was joined by others. They came over begging me to fight, saying positively that I would easily beat my opponent. The honour of the school seemed to be at stake. If I didn't fight the Harrovian it would be a moral defeat for Eton. I wanted no part of their brawling, for it had nothing to do with me. I refused their pleas, got up and walked away with shouts of 'Yella!' following me all the way. I have always felt that it was because of my colour that they wanted me to fight and were sure that I would win – because of their certainty that Negroes were stronger than whites.

At £684 a year, Eton was one of the most expensive public schools in Britain. And being one of the most populous, it was reputed to be the richest. A general discussion would take place now and again in rooms about all this, and everybody used to express their opinion that Eton, therefore, could enjoy many more advantages than any other school. Like most Etonians, I was confidently sure that no other school had such good traditions and privileges as Eton, and from this point of view, and that of the school's great fame, I felt very proud to be an Etonian. To get an idea of Eton's wealth, one only had to look at the magnificence of the 'S'-shaped swimming pool, running as the second largest in Britain. Every day in the summer it was full of hundreds of screaming creatures mobbing with relish. And there was the New Theatre, completed by my last year and used for film shows and school plays, both of which had formerly been held in the School Hall. Situated by some school buildings off Common Lane nearest to the swimming pool, it could seat 400 people, and was said to be the best and most expensive amateur theatre in Britain.

Eton seemed to have made its own kind of impact on the outside world. There was no doubt that people believed we were symbols of perfect gentlemen in the making, pure in thought, word and deed. Take the hundreds of tourists who flocked in during the weekends, particularly in the summer, taking pictures of boys and buildings. There was no doubt that they believed that seeing Etonians in their unique uniforms fulfilled their dreams of seeing their children grow up in the same traditions and ideals that nourished us. All this was the wrong image of the Etonians. We weren't always well behaved, and I wouldn't have said we were any better behaved than any other public school. Mischiefs occurred which probably would have made members of the public gasp in wide-eyed disbelief, then swallow what would feel like a small boulder – probably a gulp!

An example was an incident which took place in the Lent of my fourth and final year at the school. It was one afternoon on a Sunday, another of those mild but depressing days. I was in a boy's room in another house near the High Street. The room was big and unmercifully decorated with pictures of attractive, semi-nude girls, and the window looked out at other houses. Four of us were present, occupying all the seats there were. The other three boys were all my size, older and about a year senior, and all were the typical rough and mischievous types with thick, tously hair. I found them a most friendly bunch: they greatly admired my ability at games and respected all blacks for the same reason.

I quietly listened to them noisily engage in a foul-mouthed conversation, until the word 'masturbation' was mentioned. And just to test their reactions, I pretended not to know what the word meant and asked its meaning. They couldn't believe it, and were pretty amused.

'Well, Dillibe,' said John, clearing his throat and trying to become serious; 'don't you know how to derive sexual pleasure by yourself?' He was a snub-nosed fellow with high shoulders, and the most mischievous of the lot.

'Oh don't talk rot!' I replied. 'How can you do that? It's impossible!'

There was then a long pause, in which their whole bodies shook convulsively with laughter. I, too, was enjoying it all. 'Okay then, how do you do it?' I asked as they cooled down. 'Tell me.'

'So you've never masturbated in your life?' asked Peter, the owner of the room.

'No,' I lied.

The astonishment was overwhelming. I asked again to be told how it was done. They looked at one another and burst out laughing.

'You tell him, John!' shouted the other two. 'You're the expert.'

John protested but finally agreed. He braced himself and, smiling mischievously, somewhat nervously told me in a few sentences how to masturbate with the hands. We listened with amusement.

'That's impossible.' I persisted after he finished. 'You can't get an ejaculation that way. I'm sorry, you just can't. Only with women, there's no other way.'

Of course, we conflicted over that point. I was able to put on such a convincing show of ignorance that they really believed me. The next question – how could they make me believe?

'Show me,' was my prompt reply. 'Demonstrate and let me see.'

This, I truly didn't expect to happen. I was expecting that I would have to confess soon that I had been kidding all along. But to my amazement my request was met. First, amid their laughing, they just didn't know what to say. They kept refusing me, and I kept saying I wouldn't believe otherwise. It took a noisy five minutes before the hands pointed to John again. Again he bellowed in feigned protest but finally agreed.

'You'll find, Dillibe,' he said, 'that this can only be enjoyed in privacy. It would be difficult to get an orgasm with people present and watching you. So if you lot don't stare, I might be able to produce something.'

We agreed and I chatted normally with the other two as if he wasn't present, while he took out his penis and started to manipulate it. We continued like this for ten minutes until he stopped, and uttering sprays of laughter, said, 'I'm sorry, Dillibe, but I can't work myself up into enough excitement.'

'Well you've certainly got a big enough rise,' interrupted the third boy. That got him a good laugh.

'Oh shut up,' replied John, slightly embarrassed. 'However, Dillibe, as you can see, I have produced a little sperm.'

It was now my turn to laugh, and I did so loudly, and

mockingly. I confessed to them that I had been pulling their legs all along. And they took it in good fun.

There was no doubt that the other two would have been too ashamed to demonstrate for me. John was very popular because he thrived on laughter at his own expense. He knew his good friends, and in their presence would go to extremes to cause amusement on himself. I visited them again another Sunday afternoon to find them mobbing in John's room, which was also well decorated with pictures of semi-nudes. Another boy was there, posted outside the door to watch that nobody should come in. But I was allowed in. John was having the time of his life. He was struggling entirely naked on his bed with the two boys tickling him and throwing off his bed clothes. And he seemed to be enjoying it judging by his howling laughter. He had been apparently trying to get an afternoon siesta when his friends burst in. I was loudly greeted when I entered.

'He'll give you ten bob if you'll play with him, Dillibe,' I was told.

'Shut up!' laughed John, 'it's not true!' And he tried to cover his body with the bed clothes.

I stood and watched in amusement while they played with him for a few minutes before leaving him to continue his siesta. When I asked how he had come to be naked, I was told that he was one of those people who liked to sleep like that.

One thing I might just add is that they were all members of Debate, supposed to be more responsible Etonians, which makes the two incidents sound more unbelievable. I myself was also in Debate: I had got in the previous term.

Thus, Etonians were not absolutely perfect in their behaviour. Punishments were there to help make us nearer to perfect, most feared of them being beating, but mischief was always abundant all the same.

Beating was a commonplace when I first went to Eton, though it diminished in ferocity while I was there. Apart from House Captains, other authorities who beat boys were the Headmaster, Lower master and the 'Pops'. Housemasters rarely beat and there were only a few isolated cases of that occurring. They left all the beating to the House Captains. The Headmaster and Lower master used the birch and ordinary canes, but the birch was abolished about two terms after I went there. 'Swiping' was the boys' name for birching – a punishment for offences like smoking, cheating, drinking and homosexuality. It was a flogging – the strokes delivered across your bare skin; and it was delivered not so much because of the pain at the time, but because of what came later – little bits of twigs stuck into the skin, which had to be pulled out.

The Headmaster, with his beatings, used the cane. I understood from some boys who had been beaten by him that they had to take down their underwear, and this was not liked. Freckled Edward Wood was one of the Headmaster's 'victims'. He was a sociable sixteen-year-old of 6ft 4in., fair and very thin, and was in one of my divisions in my last term. He had been beaten for smoking and drinking in his house. I paid a social visit to his untidy room one afternoon in my last term as he was busy arranging piles of photos on his table, which he had taken himself. (Photography was his hobby and he developed his own negatives in a dark room inside Alington Schools, which only members of the Photographic Society could use.) Flicking his hair back, he said that the beating had been very painful, but he particularly complained that at his age he was beaten on his bare bottom. He felt, however, that he deserved the beating, but objected to the undignified posture of exposing his bare bottom.

I agreed with him. I didn't think it was right for someone his age to be beaten like that at all. I considered it was best suited to small children, and then only from their own parents.

The Pops, whom I mentioned just now, were self-electing school prefects, easily distinguishable from an ordinary Etonian by their black and white checked trousers, gaudy mixed-coloured waistcoats and stick-ups. They were called the Eton Society, although they had no official sanctions. They were highly privileged. They could stop a fag in the streets and send him on errands, walk into any house and give a boy-call, and fine or beat a boy for offences outside his house – offences like a disgraceful appearance, rudeness to a member of the public, mobbing and eating in the streets. Their fines were never below a half-crown and never more than ten shillings, and the offenders would have to put the money in the Pop's bedroom by whatever time the Pop gave. Their beating (called Pop-tanning) was carried out in Pop-room which was inside a building on the High Street. There they congregated, held discussions and watched television in the evenings. Offenders would be summoned by a note on their house racks a day or two after their offences, and the beating would take place later in the afternoon.

There were about sixteen Pops a term, and as (unlike House

Captains) none of them needed anybody's permission to beat a boy, they were more feared. I can say categorically that it was because of them that the general behaviour outside houses was much better than inside; for they always seemed to suddenly appear without warning. And as the public could only form their opinion of Eton boys when they were outside their houses, it can be said then that the Pops were the most helpful authorities in fulfilling the public's idea of Etonians being perfect gentlemen. Fortunately I was always able to keep out of their way.

As I have said, the two greatest privileges were having your own room and messing. One good thing about the rooms was that a boy didn't have to occupy the same room all his life at Eton. Every two or three terms he could move into another room if he wanted. After prayers at the end of term, the House Captain-to-be for the following term would visit boys' rooms, in academic seniority, with a list of the available rooms that boys could choose to move into. I changed rooms five times, the normal number, and every one of my rooms was decorated with pictures of airliners and leaving-photographs of former friends and acquaintances. The latter was the most common form of decoration in boys' rooms.

The other privilege, messing, was one I came to hate by the middle of my first term, after first being really impressed with the idea of it. To start with, my relationship with my two almost forgotten mess mates, Charles Coaker the mouse face, and Henry Lawrence the dreamer, became bad. We spent a great deal of the time arguing about whose turn it was to clear or to buy food. But the main reason that I hated messing was because it was a rather expensive affair. I found that one of the things a boy mostly had to spend his money on was food for his mess. Though this was a popular tradition, I didn't fancy the idea of it at all. One of the worst aspects of the messing system was that some boys could afford to eat more and better than others. Although the uniform of the school was designed to maintain a certain uniformity, the standard of food different boys could supply for their messes was a direct reflection of their pockets or their father's pockets, and many boys were embarrassed to eat with those whose money seemed limitless. That could almost be said for me and my mess mates. Their money seemed limitless, and on top of that their parents came to take them out several weekends, once or twice bringing food to load up our sock box — cereals, cakes, biscuits, soup, eggs, jam, etc. But the case was different for me. My guardian, being a clergyman, couldn't make it at the weekends. So I was never brought food. A boy didn't only buy what he wanted for tea, but what the whole mess decided on as well. And the demands of my mess mates were such that the £3 10s account I had at Rowland's (one of the tuck shops), expected to see me through the term, finished around the middle of term, although helped a little by my own personal spending. Naturally we always wanted to eat something different, and we always had a very big tea. Not only the usual things mentioned already, but ice-cream and specimen sizes of tinned food, like baked beans, spaghetti, ravioli, fruit and suchlike. Usually we each bought food once a week, and my average spending was over ten shillings a time. Much as I always enjoyed all the food, I could never have believed messing would mean spending so much money, and I wasn't happy about it at all.

I often tried to shirk having to buy food, and this got me into my mess mates' bad books. It was the cause of most of the arguments we had, and I never got away with my attempted shirk. As they were buying more than I was, I never had the courage to tell them that I was finding this too expensive, for I felt sure it would be received in bad taste. Our relationship was worsened by my silence at times. The extravagance of messing annoyed me so much that I kept thinking about it and hardly spoke. My silence would cause them to ask why I was so quiet, followed in reply by an angry outburst from me as to why shouldn't I be silent.

'No need to get so bad-tempered,' would come the reply, 'we only asked. You're just being a bit unsociable, that's all.' An argument would follow.

With my Rowland's account finished, I found to my annoyance that I was having to spend from my own £4 pocket money provided by my guardian. In the dame's sitting-room after lunch every Monday, the boys noisily got into a disorganized queue to collect five shillings each from her. This pocket money went on our parents' accounts, and it did, I must say, help me to settle my mess expenses, and prevented me from becoming bankrupt, which nearly happened.

That was how I viewed the messing system. Great as it may have been to eat whatever one pleased for tea, I would have preferred that tea was held in the dining-room, like the other three meals. To economize I decided to mess alone the following term. As the boys noisily chose their mess mates in the house library, I told the House Captain, but he refused to let me. No lower boy could do that, he said; and added that I would never make friends that way. So until I stopped fagging I had to put up with it. I messed with different boys each term and managed to get used to spending a lot of money. Thereafter I didn't mess again with anybody. If I felt hungry I occasionally got bread and butter from my boys' maid and ate in my room. What I usually did was to go down to a tuck shop and stuff myself. Only a few boys in my house do I recall who messed by themselves.

In my second year my pocket money went up to five pounds a term, and I imagine that that was the average for the school. And with the five shillings a week pocket money additional from the dame, I can say that the average capacity for spending was good. Some senior boys were on their own allowances. Their parents felt they were old enough to know what they wanted and gave them access to a bank account. And at the end of term, the boys paid all the school bills themselves, leaving the school fees and reports to be sent to their parents. I knew my father would never give me access to his account; for he knew too well I would spend indiscriminately. He was very strict about money, and particularly keen I should learn to save it. In fact, after I stopped messing he cut off my account in Rowland's which he considered unnecessary, as I was getting more than enough pocket money.

Apart from messing, another reflection of some boys' wealth was shown by some of their possessions in their rooms – guitars, cameras, electric shavers, penknives; and when in Debate, transistors, record players, a profusion of records. Only a few boys I knew actually bought record players; most boys brought them from home. These actually belonged to the boys, and were paid for by their parents. I never had any expensive goods in my room.

My only possessions really worth anything were my armchair, bootbox, ottoman and my carpet. I never had any envy for boys because of the things they possessed. Not even transistors, which most boys had when they became second year Specialists or were in Debate. I knew I could buy most of the things if I really decided to save my money in the term and in the holidays. I spent it mostly in the tuck shops. That was really the place where the average Etonian spent most of his pocket money. He would sit there reading comics, stuffing himself with sweets, drinks and light grills like eggs, chips and sausages, amid all the noise of boys mobbing and shouting at the counter, waiting to be served. This only happened in Rowland's, which was the biggest by far of the four tuck shops in the school. The others were far quieter. Only two of them actually belonged to the school, Rowland's and another called Jack's – the only one not on the High Street. The other two were independent, but boys frequented them and had accounts there.

I spent an average of ten shillings a week in the tuck shops; and together with other minor spendings, I was able to make my pocket money last the term. The place I found more expensive than any tuck shop was Christopher Tap, the school's pub, where boys over sixteen could buy beer and light grills. It was a bit farther down the High Street from Rowland's and had two fair-sized adjoining rooms decorated with pictures of Old Etonians, plus a garden where boys could sit in the summer and drink. The atmosphere was normally quite quiet with chinking glasses and laughter, and the smell was that of beer. It only lacked smoking and music to make it a typical public house. And like tuck shops, it was usually packed to the brim after games on half-days with thirsty and weary boys waiting their turn to be served. I was often down there after I was sixteen and always drank cider. I particularly mention Tap so as to show another privilege of Eton, undoubtedly very rare, of which I was greatly proud.

Chapter Five
Work and Games

The poor old masters were the only authorities who couldn't beat boys. All they could do was hand out lines or stiff essays, etc. plus a 'ticket', which was a piece of paper bearing the boy's offence and imposing punishment and was to be signed by both the boy's tutors. On top of all that the master could seriously speak to the boy's tutors in Chambers and suggest a white ticket. It was forbidden for masters to strike boys in any way, and if they did, boys had a right, traditionally, to hit back.

I witnessed a near example of this in a history division during my third year. A small, pleasant but lethargic boy, was gazing vacantly out of the window while something was being explained on the board. The master was young, big, strong and rather strict.

'Will you listen!' he bellowed, and with all his might hurled a piece of chalk, which caught the boy on the side of the head. Now very much awake, the lad counted this as an assault, and retrieving the chalk from the floor, threw it back without hesitation at the master, catching him on the back of the head.

'How dare you, boy?' he shouted.

'Well, sir, you're not allowed to strike us and in the event of your doing so, we have a right to strike back.'

'You will listen in future!' returned the master. 'Otherwise you'll find yourself in big trouble!' He muttered a few more words under his breath before turning back to the blackboard and continuing, a division full of amused faces behind him. It earned the smiling boy considerable praise and back-slapping from several other boys after the lesson for his quick-wittedness.

I myself was pretty tickled by that episode. I found it reassuring, for despite all the rumours I had heard that we could hit masters back, I was never prepared to believe it until I actually saw it happen. I was now encouraged to believe that I would dare to hit a master back; if not, certainly protest and remind him of what the tradition decrees.

I had in fact had a nasty experience with one master, a strict one who often threw chalk at inattentive boys, and me on occasions. He struck me as being colour prejudiced but I might have been wrong. During divisions, there always seemed something wicked and ominous in the way he looked at me – as if he loathed my guts. I was very conscious of this, especially when he used to fling chalk for inattention or shouted at me when I continuously got bad results for tests. This was the same with the other boys, but there was not that hateful glare at them. He often managed a smile for several of them, but I *never* received a glimmer of a smile. Perhaps I did not deserve one.

One incident which confirmed my suspicions about him occurred during early school one morning. We were in groups of three weighing mice to test the growth since a few days before. Ten minutes before the division ended we had to start packing up. It was my turn to wash out the mouse cage. It so happened that the master was in the adjoining small washroom when I entered, drying various objects. I soon had the cage washed and dried and was about to return to the division room, when he angrily pointed to an undried patch on the cage. He watched me dry it again, and as I was going towards the door, he kicked me powerfully up my backside. I must say he had chosen the right moment – when nobody could see. My immediate reaction was to turn to him resentfully and eye him enquiringly since such a trivial matter should not have deserved such a hefty kick. But I only received the usual evil glance before he turned to continue drying. Speechlessly, I walked back to my place, indignant. I believed firmly that he wouldn't have dared to deliver that kick for everybody to witness, for fear of arousing suspicion that he was prejudiced. For a long time it branded itself on my mind, and I made a great fuss about it to many boys. I felt something should be done and I wanted their advice on what I should do. I also expressed my feelings that the master concerned was colour prejudiced. Some boys were sympathetic, others not. The former advised me to complain to my housemaster. I gave this a lot of thought, but just couldn't pluck up enough courage to do so. I decided to give it another chance, and then I would, I vowed, report straight to my housemaster. The other advice was that I should hit back next time, which was the first time I heard we were allowed to do that to a master.

As it happened the master never hit me again. Though I think nothing of the incident now, I am still convinced that he was colour prejudiced. As I heard no mention whatever of his attitude from any boy in the division, I presumed that they were never aware of it.

All the racial insults I was experiencing in the school had made me very colour conscious, and I became very sensitive to the attitude of each and every master towards me. Anything unfavourable which occurred involving myself and a master, I always tried to detect the possibility of any prejudice behind it. But apart from my suspicions of one or two, none of them other than my assailant showed any bias in any visible way.

Putting aside the trouble I was having with my work, I continued to have a lot of difficulty with racial abuse during divisions because of my strong-arm tactics. I vividly recall an episode which took place one very foggy and cold morning in my first year during a biology division. We were all told to divide up into groups of threes to do an experiment on vegetable cells. There was the usual mad rush as friends made up their groups, and it ended with me being by myself. I approached a group of two working in one corner and asked if I could join them. One of them (whom I shall call Bruce) groaned at my question and turned to his partner.

'Do we want a wog, Bobby?' he asked. He was a freckled boy with glasses whose round head was a little too small for his body. We hated each other, and I was often punching him for racial abuse.

'I'm sorry, Onyeama,' his friend replied rather politely at least, 'we really do want to work together, please.'

'And in any case we don't want a wog,' Bruce blurted out scornfully.

Very much hurt, I was able to ignore the remark but was naturally needled. So I went to the master's desk and explained my predicament. As I thought would happen, he shouted to the two boys amid the vociferous din made by everybody that we were meant to be in threes not two, and that I was to work with them. Bruce groaned loudly.

'Oh, sir, must we have him?' he said.

'Yes you must, now get on with it,' replied the master.

'Okay then, come on, you bloody wog, and make sure you work bloody hard.'

We abused each other freely for the entire division and I delivered him several hard knuckle blows to the arm and chin. His friend Bobby, a fair-sized boy with wavy hair, just didn't take sides and completely kept out of it. I was glad, all the same, when that division was over.

My reason for relating that incident was so as to introduce some of the masters Eton had by looking at Dr Kramer's attitude to that situation. That master was middle-aged with glasses, tall and burly with a bushy grey moustache and thick hair parted in the middle. One may express astonishment at his calmness towards Bruce's reply to him when he said I should work with them. I wasn't particularly worried or hurt by this attitude, because I was so used to it. He was one of the many masters who were popular for their patience, leniency and good humour. That was fine, but at the time I was at Eton a wave of bad behaviour and abuse of these masters had begun, coinciding with the 'Permissive Society' outside. Boys were flagrantly rude to them and generally went out of their way to be as unpleasant as they could. The result was that the masters were forced into a live-and-let-live attitude, which made things bad for me too, for though they were obviously disapproving of those who racially taunted me in their classes, they did little about it. I could understand therefore the great pressure these masters were under, and I never felt any bitterness towards them for not being stern when I was abused. I found all of them jolly friendly towards me. This was certainly the case with Dr Kramer. Indeed in some divisions, his being one, the masters would often watch me hit one of my tormentors within reach and say absolutely nothing about it, but just try to quieten everybody down with threats of punishments.

Of course very few boys ever dared to utter blatantly prejudiced words in the presence of strict masters. A very beefy and lazy boy, nearly double-chinned and wearing glasses, was the only boy I recall who did so. It was in a French division one summer morning in my second year. Amid all the clamour from the traffic outside the open window, I had stood up to translate some prose into English. My continual mistakes and the corrections made by the master, Mr Peter Hazell, produced a comment of 'clumsy wog' from the beefy boy, uttered in the tone of a whisper. I was thrown into nervousness. My voice faltered, and I felt blood rush uncomfortably from my heart and surge into my face. Everybody must have heard the comment. Certainly Mr Hazell, who, standing at the radiator, was furthest from my abuser than anyone.

'Just a moment, Onyeama—' he interrupted. He was a tallish, fierce-looking man, whose trousers always seemed too big for his thin, straight body. A wave of uneasy silence reigned as he eyed my abuser angrily for a few seconds. 'Right, boy!' he shouted. 'You may come and get a ticket from me afterwards to be shown to your tutors. And also write out for me the complete translation of all the prose on this page by next time we meet. I will not tolerate such comment in my division.'

That certainly shook Andrew, the boy concerned, and he flushed sharply, no doubt wishing he had kept his mouth shut. He didn't usually abuse me. A rather reserved sort of boy whom the others found amusingly simple and stupid: a boy who, at least, didn't mind being teased sometimes about his fat figure. I was filled with grim satisfaction and elation when he was punished. I felt that the master had been just. But on seriously thinking about it later, I wondered if this justice had been purely hypocritical – perhaps he only did it to please me and hide any impression that he didn't really think it serious. But, again, on remembering that he was a housemaster, and that Akintola was in his house, plus his usual cheerful attitude towards me, I was encouraged to believe he genuinely was sympathetic. I also felt that perhaps, being strict as he was, he wouldn't have expected anybody to dare utter any form of abuse to another boy during a division, let alone racial abuse.

Masters themselves could also make things awkward for me, without trying. An unfortunate association of words by them was enough to set everyone off. I don't mean the occasion in my last year when, during an English literature division, a big, chubby-faced master with glasses made me blush three shades darker and feel nervous. He was reading a novel to the division and said 'the wogs begin at Calais'. There were numerous glances in my direction and the inevitable grins and smirks.

'Onyeama's blushing,' whispered one boy, which earned him a few giggles. I pretended to be amused, though I was pretty embarrassed. I had no hard feelings about the matter; because the lenient, young master was only reading what he saw and seemed not to realize what he said. The master who really made me feel awkward was the Lower master, Mr Frederick Coleridge. He became Vice-Provost after my second year: a strict master with blue eyes as penetrating as those of a hawk, and a very hoarse voice. I was in his Latin division my first Michaelmas term. One cold and foggy afternoon he was teaching us the different declensions of nouns and adjectives with the same endings. Rather stupidly in the circumstances, he chose the word *niger*, which of course produced a room full of silently grinning faces. Something inside me did a triple somersault. Self-consciousness swept through me, tautening every nerve, and I just wished I could vanish. The result of someone being asked to decline the word was often passed on to me in the streets and in division rooms when boys shouted 'Niger, Nigra, Nigrum! Wog, Wogra, Wogrum!' Most of the blame for this must rest with the Lower master, who dwelt on the word so long. A little hurt, I felt that he should have had the foresight to consider the possible embarrassment I might be faced with should he spend so long over the word, knowing that I was the only black in the division. Other masters showed rather more tact.

Despite what many think and others say, the rate of academic success at Eton was very high, and much of this can be attributed to the high standard of masters and the low ratio of boys to a class, somewhere in the region of one to fifteen, thus allowing individual attention. The actual teaching system was more akin to a university than to a school, with boys on the whole being left on trust to work in their own time and show it to their masters by the given day. The boys' progress therefore depended as much on their willingness to learn as the master's wish to teach. Boys tend to take patience in a schoolmaster for granted, and most of those at Eton certainly seemed to have their fair share. The general standard of behaviour in the division rooms was probably no worse than at any other public school, but there were many pretty trying boys in some of the divisions I attended. Some masters were rigid disciplinarians, others were not, and naturally the more lax among them were more popular.

An example of this was the division room of Mr John Elwick, a small, youngish biology master I was up to in the summer of my second year. His hard face, with deeply wrinkled forehead and narrow blue eyes, would give you the impression at first glance that he was strict and fierce. But no! On the contrary . . .

The usual quality of life in his division was mixed. The studious and the quiet boys would be trying to listen; others would be gazing out of the window, completely lost in dreamland; and the rest would be generally misbehaving, using obscene language, abusing each other and masters, throwing paper around, and just making a din. And Mr Elwick would continue teaching amid it all, calmly intervening occasionally. For instance, he was writing up some notes on the board for us to take down in our books one afternoon. There were several moans and grumbles.

'Oh fuck it all, sir!' shouted one fair-haired boy with a grimace. 'Do we have to copy all this down? It's so bloody boring!'

'I can't help it, I'm afraid,' replied Mr Elwick, quite unmoved, 'it's got to be done.'

'Oh to hell with work, sir!' countered the same boy. 'I wanna go home!'

'Well go home then. I don't particularly want you.'

'God, I hate you, sir! I really do!'

'I don't mind. Just keep quiet and let other boys who want to work do so.' Which was certainly one point worth mentioning. Quite often the noise-makers and the quiet ones conflicted and exchanged abuse, because the latter protested at being unable to concentrate for the noise.

All the noise and misbehaviour were mostly made by the same five boys in the back row of the division, all of whom were good friends and believed in safety in numbers. Other boys sometimes joined in their pranks. I remember that one of them actually asked Mr Elwick one day why he was so seldom strict or disciplinary.

'I'm just doing my duty,' Mr Elwick replied, somewhat unconcerned, 'which is to teach you. If you are not prepared to listen, that's not my concern but your own lookout.'

I don't recall any occasion when Mr Elwick gave a ticket to a boy for misbehaving, nor raised his voice in anger. He had a rather smart way of making boys become more serious and realistic without having to punish them himself: more or less an indirect way of reporting them to their tutors. Twice a week he gave us a test. And because of his great patience and leniency towards us, boys like the tomfoolers and daydreamers often didn't really bother to revise the set work for that test, and inevitably produced bad results. Mr Elwick reacted in turn without mercy: despite all the pleas and false, invalid excuses from the boys for doing so badly, he always gave a rip to every boy below forty per cent plus a request for a complete rewrite. Dismayed, the boys would only worry about the inevitable hot reactions to come from their tutors, who would without doubt threaten a white ticket if this continued. Their tutors would also soon see their bad fortnightly reports, in each of which Mr Elwick would have given an honest account of a boy's progress and behaviour.

All this made the boys revise their work a bit more thoroughly, especially as a few of them were put on white ticket and others threatened it by their tutors, but the usual bad behaviour did not really improve. And as Mr Elwick and indeed other patient masters with similar viewpoints, took it all with a pinch of salt and never seemed bothered, they did not really deserve any sympathy, I feel. I never had the courage to join in the pranks for fear that once my voice was heard, I would become the centre of racial abuse again. I normally kept silent and sometimes joined the daydreamers. The only feelings that I had for these masters was that of respect and a little envy for their patience and cool temper. The envy was because I was unable to take all the racial abuse I suffered as calmly as they took all the pranks and rudeness, and become as popular as they were.

Of course it was the stricter masters who were able to tame the boys in their divisions, and produce breathless silence as they taught. Only the noise of speeding motorcycles and planes used to disturb that silence. It was also of course with those masters that boys made better progress. One such master was plump Mr Charles Impey, a round-faced bachelor in his early forties with glasses and thin, dark hair. Of medium height, he was a Classics master. He had the speed and heat of temper of a bull and would furiously swear and mutter to himself every time a jetliner flew over low. And he only needed to see a boy daydreaming or smiling for no apparent reason, for his snappy voice to roar out threats. He gave a rip every time a boy got below half marks for a test.

Though his alarming temper made him rather unpopular with the boys, the general feeling was that it induced everybody to work much harder and better. I certainly believed so. For instance, during my second Lent term when I was in his division, history was one of the subjects I disliked and was terrible at. At the end of term, I scored sixty per cent in Trials – my highest then by thirty per cent after having attended the divisions of more lax masters, and it was one of the lowest marks in Mr Impey's division. In fact it was in the Classics subjects, which also included Latin and divinity, that I scored best for Trials that term. And I have always felt that it was due to the strict and forceful teaching of Mr Impey that I did so well. I myself didn't like him because of his temper, but, like everybody else, respected his teaching. There were a number of masters like him whose divisions I attended, perhaps not quite so hot-tempered but just as forceful.

So that was how boys progressed better with the stricter masters than with the lax ones; they were more or less *forced* to listen and learn. On the whole, I preferred being with the strict masters for one sole reason; nobody dared to racially abuse me in their divisions. Otherwise, I would have preferred the patient masters, like most boys, for I was a lazy character and didn't like work at all.

As I said earlier, my usual fortnightly positions in most subjects during my first year were within the last six – even in some of the subjects I found the easiest, which included Latin, French and divinity, though I was never actually last in any of them. Mathematics was the only subject I was able to stay in single figures; and in my first fortnight at the school, which we spent on algebra in the division I was in, I came first. But unfortunately I never achieved that again. For science and history, I was either last or one of the last three, and the same applied to geography when I started doing it after my first year. At English I was not particularly good either, but I don't recall ever coming last. I was usually about three or four places from bottom.

Until I took my 'O' levels in Michaelmas 1966, my positions in all these subjects hardly improved. Though the number of rips I was getting a term dropped from about thirteen in my first year to around nine, my academic progress generally was still bad. And it seemed that Latin, French, divinity and mathematics were the only subjects I could pass 'O' levels in – one less than the required number for a boy to remain in the school and take his 'A' levels.

It always made me feel deeply uncomfortable whenever I turned up last in the fortnightly orders, and I had a complex about it. Because, I was positive that everybody had one idea in their heads: it was of course natural – just the sort of position Africans would be expected to occupy. I was always conscious of this, and was constantly filled with a firm resolution to come anywhere but last. I must not, I felt, continue to give them this false idea of the Africans. Whenever I came last, I was always very hesitant to tell boys when they asked after divisions. But miserably I did. And occasionally there were the typical replies, like, 'Hard luck. It's not really fair on you, because you're at a sort of . . . disadvantage.' I always took it without a word in reply. I only thanked the stars that during divisions, my tormentors never drew attention to my bad progress and abused my race because of that.

It was where rips were concerned that I mostly met with this question of colour being blamed for my bad progress. One occasion I vividly remember was in our friend Mr John Elwick's biology division. I entered the division one afternoon and was only the third boy to arrive. The other two boys were by the master's desk, looking at their marks for a test we had two days before. Mr Elwick was standing there, with one of the boys, Viscount William Astor, begging him to no avail to be let off a rip he had got for the test.

'Ah Onyeama,' called Mr Elwick, looking for my exercise book among the pile on his table . . . 'I'm afraid your test wasn't up to scratch, so I've given you a rip.' I put down my other books and went to collect it from him. 'Don't worry, you're by no means the only one,' he added, as I looked at my ripped test.

'Oh sir, don't give him a rip,' Astor joined in with mock concern. 'You can't expect him to be as brainy as us, sir.' He was a rather handsome fellow with long, dark hair and narrow eyes. Slim and tallish, he was argumentative and abusive, but wasn't snobbish, unlike some of the peers at the school. His comment infuriated me. I pushed him roughly on the chest.

'You say that again, Astor,' I warned viciously, 'and I'll smash your jaw open!'

'What's wrong with you?' he replied, affronted. 'I was only being bloody kind!'

'Now if you two must fight,' interrupted Mr Elwick, 'please go outside. Not in here.'

I sighed irritably and returned to my seat as more boys noisily entered. There was just nothing else I could say. Yes, the implications were there all the time: Africans were simply thick. This was rubbed into me more times than I can possibly remember. It came from the constant, built-in arrogance and ignorance with which my fellows approached everything. This was a part of the tragic legacy of colonialism in Africa.

The masters in whose divisions I always did badly never showed in any visible way that their beliefs as to why I was so thick were similar to the boys'. Yet they made no allowances or let me off rips. One belief – as shown in the typical comments they would write in my reports: that I was finding this subject extremely difficult, and they were not sure if I was understanding their teaching – was definitely to be associated with my origins. This to me meant that they assumed I was faced with a lot of anxiety, caused by my being totally different from the others, and this was enough to lessen my ability to concentrate. This on the whole was not correct. It only applied when I encountered racial abuse in some divisions; for, being greatly hurt by them, I was thus unable fully to concentrate on the teaching. (But putting that aside, I know I still wouldn't have improved in my positions.)

My housemaster's interpretation of those reports was that I found difficulty in understanding the English language: a possible implication I had never thought of. Just after my first year he brought this up a few times when he visited me at night, asking if I was having difficulty with English and understanding the masters when they taught. I knew that certainly wasn't the case, and I always said so. Having lived in England since 1959, I had, in my opinion, quite a mastery of the English language, and I always liked to imagine that I found it no more difficult than the average Etonian, nor was my vocabulary any worse. My spoken English wasn't as good, admittedly, in the sense that anybody listening to me on tape would know I wasn't English, but they would never believe I was an African, for my accent wasn't English or African – it was just an adopted accent. I was more of a fast talker and sometimes gabbled. So my housemaster, who was always very candid and concerned in his approach, used to ask what my difficulty could then be? Somewhat shyly, I used to answer that I just wasn't good at work.

'Nonsense!' he once replied reassuringly. 'Nobody can say he isn't good at work. Anybody can make good progress if he tries. Some of your reports often say you're inattentive in school. I'm sure you can improve if you're determined to do so and put in a bit more effort.'

He was smiling as he spoke. There was something very patronizing in the way he spoke and smiled, and I was encouraged to believe that he wouldn't have been so kind to a white Etonian. I nodded after he finished, with the knowledge that this was an empty nod. True enough I was often inattentive, and I knew that I would continue like that. I disliked the idea of having to try hard and I couldn't see myself really making any better progress. I have always felt that a little of the blame for my inattention and poor progress should go to my housemaster, because he never put me on white ticket. Knowing that I was continually being inattentive, and as a result made bad progress, and as white ticket was especially supposed to deal with such boys, why then didn't he and my Classical tutor when they met every day in Chambers, decide to put me on white ticket? That I knew would certainly have been effective. I only regret that I never put these questions to him when he used to approach me in my room about my work. The idea did come to my mind, but I never knew how to say it, nor had the courage. I felt it would have been interesting to hear what his reasons were. What I was really hoping for was a chance to politely express my strong suspicion, and distaste, of his composite belief that my race and colour influenced my work, and that as a result he patronized me. I'm convinced that that was the cryptic truth, and I felt it was a more convincing reason than his idea of my incomprehension of English, and also the question of my inattention in division rooms.

And finally regarding the white ticket: I was positively sure that it was my housemaster's idea much more than my Classical tutor's that I should be exempt. As I mentioned earlier, the latter was much stricter, and left to himself, I strongly suspected that he would have gone ahead and put me on white ticket. He never patronized me in any way, and seemed less sympathetic than my housemaster. I felt that my housemaster always managed to influence him and was able to form an agreement with him that I should be spared from white ticket. My feelings now regarding all this are still the same.

It was when my 'O' levels came that I was able to prove to everybody that I, and therefore all Africans, were not so stupid. A few terms after I joined the school, Eton introduced a new 'O' levels system. Instead of taking all subjects in one go, boys were now to take only three or four subjects in their second year. The subjects were Latin, French, English language and Maths, which were considered to be the easiest papers. This method was supposed to give a boy more time to prepare for the more difficult subjects the following year. I took Latin, French and English in summer 1966, and passed them quite easily, except for English where I scored the exact pass mark. The results had come in the holidays (while I was in Oxfordshire). I just eagerly looked forward to the beginning of the following term. I was overjoyed and wanted to compare my results with the boys in my divisions. One by one the boys returned from home, all fresh and healthy, full of smiles and good humour. Then up to their rooms to deposit and unpack their baggages, and later downstairs again to the house-library to find out from the booklets on the table what were their work timetables and divisions for the term, and what books they had to order. Apart from their holiday activities, the main topic of the boys in my divisions was of course their 'O' level results. Inside their rooms and in the house-library they discussed it, and when I made it known that I scored three passes, I was greeted with loud, hearty praises! At one time, about twenty boys were noisily assembled in the Library waiting for a chance to see the work booklets. I quietly approached a small group cheerfully discussing their results in one corner, joined in and revealed my results. 'Did you?!' they all shouted, 'bloody well done, Charlie! That's bloody good!'

Timothy Elliot announced it to the whole room. 'Say Charlie passed in all, folks! He got three "O's"!' General congratulations followed from those much senior and junior to me. After all, just about the whole house knew about my continual bad progress. I shyly told Elliot to shut up.

Most of the candidates in my house passed all the subjects they took, and of all of them only one boy scored below one. But, of course, nobody else received half the hearty congratulations that I got, or had their results broadcast.

Outside my house it was the same story. For two days a good dozen boys, mostly those senior to me by a year, approached me in the streets and in tuck shops, and congratulated me. 'Is it true you got three "O's"?' was the typical sort of question, followed after my reply by 'My God! Well done!' And in division rooms it was again the same thing. In most of the six divisions I attended on that second day of term my results were shouted out, and together with those loathsome ape noises I received, for a change, praises from nearly everybody – even from my main tormentors.

My feelings towards all the praises were mixed. It relieved me, at least, that everybody had seen I wasn't so thick. But even a few usually stupid boys in my divisions who themselves scored three or four hardly received any praise. Why then me in particular? It was no doubt because my continual bad progress at work had prompted everybody to believe I would fail, and my results were thus an anticlimax. But I felt that the main reason was that being an *African* who had shown no marked academic prowess, everybody had been more than positive that I could not pass. So I found that I had more distaste for the praise than pleasure, when I stopped to think of the implications: for me, an African, pretty good! But I never took any offence. I felt it would just be in very bad taste; for obviously the boys didn't realize the implications. I always smiled and accepted the praise with thanks.

About four boys I knew passed nothing and a few others got one pass. It was the rather hostile way some of them eyed me in division rooms, and ignored me completely that caused me to strongly suspect an air of envy invading them because I had beaten them. I noticed this especially when I approached them as they lolled around the clamorous divisions, and politely enquired about their results. It was always a sharp reply expressed irritably and rather hesitantly before they stalked off without another word. I cannot describe how delighted I really felt, for now I obviously didn't seem so stupid to them.

Thank goodness the boys' reactions to my results were not the same amongst any masters except for one. My housemaster and Classical tutor were happy at least that I passed English language: they hadn't expected that to be one of my passes, and it surely must have reassured my housemaster that I wasn't finding English difficult to understand, though he didn't say so.

The one master whose reaction at my results was like the boys' was Mr Charles Chamier. He was a double-chinned mathematics master in his late fifties with wire glasses set on a broad, square face. A little over six feet, he had a huge nose and had a mannerism of licking his lower lip. He was a housemaster and his division room was held in his house. A charming and witty master but a strict disciplinarian, he had already taken my division for two terms. However, three days after the term began, we had our first mathematics division in the morning. He entered with his heavy footsteps and exchanged greetings with us.

'Welcome to a new term!' his deep, rapid voice boomed, as he placed his books on his desk. 'Before we dash off into mathematics, I would like to give my congratulations to those of you who scored three passes in the "O" levels, especially Onyeama, who brilliantly scooped up the lot; for him I think it's most encouraging. Now if he and the rest of you go hard, you should be just as successful next year when the real stinkers come up. Those of you who got nothing – I think there were only three of you in the division – had better pull your socks up if you expect to remain in the school after next year.' He went to the blackboard and vigorously started to wipe it with the duster on the ledge. 'Now let's go hard at some maths,' he continued, 'and see if some of you can't be successful at that as well.'

I thanked him for his 'compliment' and managed an insincere smile of appreciation. That 'compliment' didn't produce any reaction from any boy, but it tore through my heart like an arrow. I wasn't so much angry as hurt, for I knew he meant well, but was obviously ignorant of his abusive implication. I was very much aware of his great admiration for me both as a person and a sportsman. On several occasions when I was last to leave at the end of his divisions, he spent several moments asking how I was getting on, and about my family and Nigeria. He also used to praise and flatter me considerably for my prowess at games, and express his great impression of me after watching me in action at football, cricket and boxing. I was aware that he was never as kind and praising to any other boy in the division, and I certainly felt very much flattered. Even during divisions on a number of occasions, he continued amusing everybody with his funny, vivid descriptions of my sportsmanship. A few times he actually made statements, like, 'You Africans certainly have the whip over us at games, and I'm sure the boys must be alarmed and envious playing against you – especially at your size! I certainly would be!' And amid the usual laughter and voices of agreement were a few ape noises and one or two racial names uttered in subdued tones. Nobody ever dared utter them within his hearing.

How I adored and lapped up that praise – especially when he attributed my prowess to my race. I recall that once or twice after his divisions, a few boys approached me outside and said they were positive that he really admired me a lot.

I knew a number of masters who admired my prowess at games; but honestly none of them showed their admiration anything like as openly and regularly as Mr Chamier. And very few masters did I find quite so friendly. He never made any allowances for me. He didn't need to, since I was usually about fifth in mathematics fortnightly orders. And he barely gave rips, no matter how appalling a boy's work was: he simply made us correct our mistakes. The occasion he talked about the 'O' level results was the first that he showed me that his respect for Africans as sportsmen was countered by a belief that they were also stupid. But alas! one has to be prepared for sudden shocking surprises. It didn't, however, lessen my great liking and respect for him.

However, as for those three 'O' level passes, they were just the beginning: the following year would decide if I would remain in the school. My work continued as badly as usual until then with the exception of science, which I had given up, substituting geography in its place. My only chances now were divinity and mathematics. Knowing me to often produce bad results in my best subjects, my tutors were rather concerned that that might happen in these two. They kept saying so when I continued bringing rips at frequent intervals to them. And a few times when he visited at night, my housemaster candidly expressed his thoughts that I should leave the school if I failed, and have intensive tuition at a London coaching establishment. That, he felt, was the only way I could improve. This was what he wrote in my end-of-term reports to my father. And I always agreed with him that it would be a good idea. That was a common practice for 'O' level failures at Eton, and also 'A' level candidates who weren't sure they would pass or pass well enough for university.

I was always confident that I would revise thoroughly enough to fetch at least two more passes in the remaining 'O' levels, and I was never at all worried. Finally summer 1967 came. I took five more subjects, and managed to pass three of them, failing in mathematics and geography. And but for history, which became the second subject I scraped through with the exact pass mark, the other subjects were fairly easy passes. My highest grade was a '4' in English literature, Latin and divinity. I was quite shattered at my failure in mathematics and the pass in history. I had truly expected the opposite. However, I passed mathematics before I left the school, though to my astonishment, it took two more attempts. I had come to know of its significance in society and that one couldn't get many jobs without it.

The result of those 'O' levels didn't come until a week after the following term began. And when they did arrive, how greatly stunned and confounded a good many people were at my results is hard to describe. Truly, it circulated the school like wildfire! The reactions were as before, only more widespread and producing more distaste. As well as the praise from all over the school came remarks that really got me. An example was in Christopher Tap, some days after the results. It was before tea one half-day, and there were a fair number of boys inside. I was in a small queue at the counter waiting to be served, and neither the voices nor the numerous sounds of cutlery on crockery prevented me from hearing the mention of my name in the adjoining room by Charles Yorke-Long. He was at a table with four friends. After I got my drink I approached them.

'I seem to hear my name pronounced with dead accuracy,' I said cheerfully, and asked politely what he had said.

He was a very argumentative boy whom I had often clashed with in division rooms. A tallish, small-nosed fellow who was one of about seven boys who scored below five 'O' levels and left the school that term. At my question he took a mouthful of steak and kidney pie, washed it down with some Guinness, then dithered hesitantly. Then, 'I think you'd get angry if I told you,' he said without looking at me. 'You wouldn't like to hear it.'

My curiosity was instantly roused to the zenith. I gave him my word I was prepared for the worst and wouldn't mind at all, and begged him to tell me. He swallowed another mouthful of beer and cleared his throat.

'Well,' he replied, again hesitantly and without looking at me, 'it's just that you passed your "O's" because your pass marks were lowered, and your papers were marked more leniently.'

My heart twisted over and stood still with shock. 'Where the hell did you get that idea from?' I asked pretty sharply.

'I've been hearing it from several people,' he replied.

For a moment I was speechless in paralysed disbelief. My face distorted with incredulity. Cold fury swiftly uncoiled itself from inside me; but so as not to disturb the scene, I schooled my voice to be calm but firm. His friends ate silently and looked on.

'What the hell!—Surely you don't believe that, do you?'

Raising his head, he replied honestly and quietly, 'Yes, I do.'

'You do?!'

'Yeah, I can well believe it.'

I just didn't know what to say next. A smothering sense of frustration swept over me. I completely forgot I was holding a pint of cider and I wonder I didn't drop it. I felt a harsh rebellion restricting my throat.

'Well!' I replied threateningly, 'you'd better not go spreading that round, because it isn't true. There'll be trouble for you if you do, I promise!'

'Onyeama, just go away,' he answered irritably, 'I told you you wouldn't like it.'

'You try spreading it and see,' I said, turning for the other room. 'You only believe it because you're bloody jealous that I passed and you failed.'

'Oh, just bugger off, will you, Onyeama.'

I knew it was quite ridiculous and nonsensical for anyone to suggest that the examiners were part of some vast conspiracy and fiddle to get me through. Where the rumour first started from I never knew, but never heard any more of it after my exchange with Yorke-Longe. It upset me a lot and heckled my mind for a few days, for it was a false rumour which I knew people would easily swallow. I knew it was just another case of boys' underestimation of African intelligence. As I told Yorke-Longe, he was simply jealous. I knew it and so did he. I believed the truth was that to be beaten by a black person shamed him, particularly as he normally beat me in most subjects, and to redeem himself, he gladly wanted to believe the rumour.

He was by no means the only jealous boy. The other failures seldom spoke to me again, and the same applied to a number of boys who overall got five 'O' levels. But their jealousy ran down in time. These boys included those up to three terms senior to me, and a few of them were in my house, where the results had been good with no failures. I didn't think it was so much jealousy that haunted the failures at my beating them as embarrassment and humiliation.

When the final results came, I had somehow foreseen that some sort of false rumour would be conjured up as to how I could have passed. Apart from the stated example was the response from several boys that I must have cheated – no other explanation seemed possible. And I suspected that that was the general feeling amongst most of the boys, despite their praises. I cannot honestly remember the amount of times I met with those kind of questions. 'Tell me, Onyeama, you cribbed, didn't you?' or 'Just how did you do it, Onyeama? Really, did you crib?' Though my enquirers were usually smiling, their questions were sincere. For a week they asked me this – in my house, on football fields, in divisions, everywhere. Categorically I always denied it. 'I worked for them just like anybody else, damn it!' was my typical furious reply. It would have hurt me more if I had asked and been told why the hell I shouldn't have passed, and I never did. There could only have been one answer.

Dillibe Onyeama, aged fourteen.

School yard, Eton College.

Dillibe's House Group, 1965.

Opposite top: Dillibe talks to
the late Brigadier Ogundipe at
a reception held at the Nigerian
Centre in London, 1970.

Right: Dillibe with his brother
and friend on the steps of St Peter's,
Rome, in 1966.

Dillibe was a member of the Eton College Junior Athletics Team, pictured here in 1966.

In 1965 Dillibe became a member of the Eton College Boxing Team.

Above: Eton College's Second Eleven Cricket Team, 1968, celebrate another victory.

Below: The Second Eleven Cricket Team pictured before the match.

The cast of the Eton College production of *Billy Budd*, summer 1968.

Actor Dillibe in the College production of *Antony and Cleopatra*, 1968.

Dillibe pictured with his step-mother and younger brothers in Holland in 1968.

Below left: Dillibe boxing in a sparring match against a London Club, 1965.

Below right: Dillibe and friends listen to orators at London's Hyde Park Speakers' Corner, 1971.

Dillibe in his national costume in London, 1971.

A few of the masters who had taught me heartily congratulated me in the streets, not to my surprise. But none of them at least made an implication like Mr Chamier did the previous year. Both my tutors were at least prepared to accept that I had worked hard to pass and had, therefore, passed by my efforts. But I have always lived under the belief that in other masters' minds was the suspicion that I must have cheated.

I cannot describe how the reaction to my results got on my nerves. It caused me to lie in bed till well past midnight on a number of nights thinking about them. And eventually I concluded that something should be done about it. I had first thought of writing a strong letter of complaint to the local weekly newspaper, *The Windsor, Eton and Slough Express*, complaining of the way white people underrated African academic ability, using my experiences at Eton as an example. But I was put off at the thought of getting into serious trouble as a result. Instead I wrote a long, less cynical letter a few weeks after the results, about African and British education. I praised British education, said that Britain of course offered better education, and that it was due to their efforts that Nigeria, for example, was improving so much. But I expressed my distress at the way white people voiced their poor opinion of African academic ability, and pointed out that if an African boy with average intelligence and his British counterpart were together under the same master, the African would most probably do better, because for him it would be so important, and the chance of a lifetime.

The letter was published. But hardly anybody read the local newspaper in the school. I showed it to a number of boys in my house: in the big School Library (which was in the same building as School Hall) a few boys came across it; my housemaster, a few other masters, and people like shopkeepers read it. None of them had anything to say about it, except that it was interesting and a 'good write-up'. They did not take me up on any of the points I made. However, one can be quite sure that the letter in no way altered their views.

Once a boy passed 'O' levels at Eton, thus becoming a Specialist, his academic life changed. He would have decided the previous term which two or three subjects he would like to take for 'A' levels (assuming he was to get the required amount of 'O' levels to take 'A's) and those subjects he would have to study. This of course meant that the amount of divisions he would need to attend a week would be considerably minimized – from the previous thirty to as few as twelve. And where he had no divisions, he compulsorily observed a quiet 'reading school' in his room while the non-Specialists toiled away in their classrooms: there he could either read or prepare set work.

He would have seen the last of his Classical tutor. The previous term he would have found himself a master he knew and favoured who taught any of the 'A' level subjects he was to study. This master was a Specialist's equivalent to a Classical tutor, and was called a 'Modern tutor'. The difference was that the former was chosen for the boy just before he entered the school, and the latter he had to choose himself and was to remain with until he left the school.

A Specialist, of course, now had to work much harder than in the past if he really wanted to get to university. I found this out and I did not like it at all. The hard work and great amount of reading that had to be done simply knocked the wind out of me, and I just didn't feel I could do it, nor did I want to do it. I was helplessly overcome by boredom and laziness, and I just deplored work more and more and the whole idea of school.

I specialized in French and English literature, and I'm afraid to say that my progress was by no means better than before: it was worse. French, a subject I was once good at, became very much the opposite. I was now getting very few rips – about three a term. This was because I was only studying two subjects, and most of the masters I now had didn't give rips. My fortnightly reports were not encouraging at all. I was always within the last four in both subjects, and I recall that two or three times I came last in French, but never in English.

As there were different parts to each 'A' level paper, boys found themselves up to two or three different masters for each subject. None of the masters I was up to showed much enthusiasm about my work, and each felt that I would have to make much greater effort if I was to pass 'A' levels. This was what they wrote in my reports. My housemaster was prompted to suggest strongly to my father that a coaching establishment, where there were no games or other activities but only intensive tuition, was the only answer. I would not pass, he felt, if I remained at Eton. This was my feeling, too. My father took his advice, and three terms after I became a Specialist, I left to attend a coaching establishment in London.

There isn't really much one can say about the standard of games and sports at Eton except that Eton had quite reputable qualities.

Though academic work was, of course, more important than play, the boys categorized play with the same seriousness, and this created added impetus to pursue diligently their efforts in both work and play. I had been able to keep up my success at games and sports throughout my time at the school. But what else? I was an African, wasn't I? And all niggers were good at sports! They were all stronger than white men! This was the same old story all the time. My most successful games were cricket, The Field Game and boxing. In the latter part of my time at the school I was awarded my colours in all three games. At cricket, I retained my respect as a good bowler, and also the reputation of being the fastest and most dangerous bowler in the school. I continued to strike and inflict injuries on quite a number of batsmen, causing added fear and uneasiness to a lot of people.

Though the Eleven and the Twenty-Two always played fixed games together and practised at nets, I was not, unfortunately, able to reach the team of the former. I only got into the Twenty-Two in my last summer at the school. And as well as my colours for it, I had also received my colours for the team I played in the previous year. I would most likely have made the Eleven if I had stayed on till the following summer, but as it happened, I left two terms before.

The truth of the situation was that the quality of my bowling was highly exaggerated by everybody and made to sound extraordinarily dynamic. Had I been white, and a slow bowler, that would definitely not have been the case. From time to time in different parts of the school I came across boys expressing their surprise that I was not in the Eleven. I knew this was all due to these exaggerations. The simple truth was that effective as it may have been, it was not as good as the other fast bowlers' in the Eleven, whether or not it was faster and more dangerous, and whether or not I was black.

I'm afraid I wasn't much good as a batsman at all, but I did have my moments of glory. I was just a happy-go-lucky slogger and nothing else: and one of those accurate guys who usually made contact with the balls, scoring spectacular 'sixes' and 'fours'. In my second and last year in the Junior house, I succeeded in scoring my century in one match against another house. My score was III, with eleven 'sixes' and a profusion of 'fours'. We were playing on Dutchman's Plough, and all the time I was gripped by warm, wholly pleasurable and surging joy as applause after applause went up from my side. Everybody was thoroughly enjoying it, including the opposing team (who lost). Gasps of delight resounded whenever the ball went high. I only felt sorry that matches between junior house sides were not reported in the *Eton College Chronicle*. But all the same, a good number of boys and masters heard about it, and the usual congratulations met me everywhere.

My slogging was very much liked by masters and boys – more than any other boy's I could think of. And I believed that it was more a question of sheer admiration for me than overrating the strength of black people. A black person skying the balls seemed more spectacular to everybody than a white person, whether or not his balls were sent higher.

It was during nets practices that I mostly had my chance to hit skyscrapers. And every time I went in to bat, persistent voices shouted for skyscrapers, and the boys practising in my nets deliberately bowled slow full-tosses for me to swing at. And whenever I did connect shrieks of delight resounded, plus cries of 'heads!'

'Well struck, my beautiful discus thrower!' shouted a short, bearded young master one evening in my third summer. From his nets he had watched, amid all the gasps, a high one that I had hit. And his comment was met with a good deal of laughter, and pretty amused myself, I thanked him. Throughout my time at Eton, many people's ears were being invaded by rumours about my slogging strength – once again magnified out of all proportion simply because . . .

Boxing was the sport I had come to like best. Not so much because of the sport itself, but because of the friendliness of the boys in the team. They were the most friendly lot I ever met in any game at Eton.

One of the small gyms was used for boxing training after games on half-days, and usually about a dozen of the twenty or so boxers turned up to train. Unlike other games, boxing introduced a different approach. We were not pushed into rigid training procedures nor into serious attacks; nor did we abide by any set rules of behaviour. We were free, with a jolly old trainer to coach us. He was one of the gym staff (who weren't officially counted as masters and didn't wear stick-ups), and was himself a one-time amateur heavyweight boxer; a grey humorous man with a slight cockney accent, whom everybody chatted freely to in all kinds of languages.

I started boxing in my second Lent term, and was pronounced by many to be the heavyweight champion of the school. I was

called this because I was always the only heavyweight at the
school by a long way, beginning from twelve stone and reaching
over thirteen by the time I left Eton. Boxing was only popular as
a spectator sport. The twenty boxers fought for Eton against
other schools, so there were no champions as such amongst them.
Only for the voluntary School Boxing Competition, which took
place annually and saw about 300 competitors, were there champ-
ionships for the weights. But I never entered for the competition,
for so many boys at heavyweight class used to beat up one another
so badly, that the Headmaster brought the heaviest weight limit
down to eleven stone my first year. So Heavyweight Champion
was more of a nickname than anything else really, which I accepted
with great pleasure. I knew it was also because of my colour that
I received that nickname. During training, everybody used
greatly to admire my Cassius Clay style of boxing and adored
watching me spar and punch the bags. They were always anxious
to see me in action against other schools. 'None of them would
stand a chance against *you*!' was a remark I heard often. 'You'd
mangle them!'

'Well, this is the game of his people,' Mr Kelly, the trainer,
replied a few times with a grin.

I only had five fights in my time at Eton, but managed to win
them all. I had so few because boxing's popularity had greatly
deteriorated in most schools. All the big, heavy boxers had packed
up, and it was very difficult finding opponents for my weight class.
However, except for my first fight in which my opponent had to
retire at the end of the second round with a badly cut lip, I won
the rest of my fights on points. There was always an added air of

excitement among the spectators when I stepped in the ring, and everybody, especially the other Eton boxers, expected me to be the winner. And every fight that I won, I was congratulated more than anybody else. It was accepted as right and proper that I had won: after all, I *was* a Negro!

The Field Game was the only form of football I found success at after my first year, and I earned the nickname 'The Rock' from the *Eton College Chronicle* because of my powerful return of the ball. Throughout my time at the school I retained my reputation of being the school's most powerful kicker, and, as I said before, I only enjoyed playing in house matches so as to show off my kicks to the spectators and get applauded for it. Otherwise, like most of the school, I didn't like The Field Game much.

I was lazy at games as well as work. Games which I was good at, but which I didn't especially favour, I never took seriously. It meant too much effort. After my success at football my first year, I completely lost interest in it and never cared to play in any more school games. I opted for the alternative and started playing in the occasional unimportant house and inter-house games, and got all the attention for my kicks there instead!

The same applied to the hundred-yards sprint. Throughout my time, when I was up at the running tracks to watch athletics matches, a number of athletes and a few masters always suggested strongly that I should take up the hundred yards again. They were positive that I would do very well if I bothered to come up and practise often. This was something I thought over at times. I was quite a fast runner, and I was good at the hundred yards. But again it meant exerting myself and I didn't want to do it. That was the only kind of running at which I excelled. At long distances I was a total failure and I kept right away from them. I never had the stamina that they demanded, and, moreover, I did not have the interest.

I was able to represent the school for athletics, however, and that was in the Junior team in my second year for throwing the discus only. And this was another case where boys' over-estimation of the strength of Negroes became apparent. I had never handled the discus before and didn't do very well against other schools. I never seemed to be able to hurl it more than ninety feet. I was instructed mostly by boys of my own age. One of them was a short, but powerfully built boy named Richard Bancroft. He was a fair boy over a year senior to me, who became Captain of boxing in my last year. A superb and very friendly athlete. We were practising one mild half-day before an audience of small boys, the running tracks as usual colourfully speckled with athletes in whites or track-suits ardently practising their events. Bancroft had no problem in hurling the discus over a hundred and ten feet . . . Not a word from our small audience. Then it was my turn, and the whispers from the audience were quite audible. 'Here! Watch this black chap. Watch him!' And with all my weight behind it, I could throw the discus no more than ninety feet. Yet there were gasps of astonishment. 'Golly! Look at that! . . . My God!' They were filled with admiration and awe, and I was filled with pride and conceit.

It so happened that I succeeded in getting into the finals for the school athletics competition at the end of term. This time the audience was much bigger and included a number of boys from my house. Luck took a hand for me. A tremendously strong cross-wind was blowing, and was hampering the throws of the other junior competitors. Nobody could make use of it to their satisfaction, and the longest throw was only a hundred and nine feet. My own longest was eighty – until the last one. Then, to my delight, it was caught by the wind and sailed in a long banana curve. Just under a hundred and eleven feet, and the winner. It was nothing but sheer fluke! But the spectators thought differently. Amid their heart-warming applause, I was heavily patted on the back by several.

'It was yours all the way, Charlie!' they flattered me. 'I was waiting for that. I knew you could easily win it!'

So that was me at Eton. Black, and therefore stupid! Thick-skinned, and only to be reviled: yet stronger physically than a white man. I am afraid to say that that was the Etonian outlook, and I doubt very much if anything will change it. I believe that my contemporaries have made up their minds. When they become politicians, business tycoons, or Cabinet Ministers even, their feelings will be the same. It is possible that they may learn to dissemble, but those feelings will not change. And how on earth they will get on dealing with African states, I really don't know.

Chapter Six
Me and the People at Eton

Remarkably enough, it was two South Africans at Eton whom I remember for not jeering at my colour; and it may sound ironical if I say that it was their friendship that I have always particularly remembered. Having foreign students to study for a term or two was a tradition at the school, so I thought little of seeing a new face in my English division the second day of my last Lent term. The division room was very large. It was on the third floor of a building called New Schools; and its numerous windows offered a gorgeous view of Windsor Castle and its picturesque surroundings. The new boy was quietly looking out of the window amidst the usual mobbing and shouting when he was approached by a tall, grinning figure with glasses.

'Are you one of the new guys from one of those funny countries?' the latter asked. His name was Bell, a witty and intelligent ruffian with collar-length hair, who was no friend of mine.

'Yes,' the new arrival replied, totally unmoved.

'Which country?'

'South Africa.'

I was sitting silently nearby, observing all this. I froze in my pants, and my heart gave a great thump. Apartheid, I thought at once. The words go together: South Africa – apartheid. So he is from a country where the blacks and whites loathe each other. Is he himself a black man hater? Will he explode if I dare approach him? These thoughts travelled in my mind as rapidly as a drowning man sees the whole panorama of his life. I got up and moved nearer.

'So you're a South African are you?' I asked in a tone of interest, smiling.

'Yeah,' he replied. 'And you're an American?' He had a strong Afrikaans accent.

'No. Actually I'm from Africa too. Nigeria. Or Biafra if you like.'

'Oh yes?' He seemed surprised. 'You speak like an American.'

'No,' I laughed, 'I'm African through and through.'

We would have continued but for the interruption of the boy who started the chat. I knew he was trying to make trouble.

'Now don't start fighting you two,' he said loudly, 'you're in England now, not Africa.'

I stayed silent, feeling damned embarrassed. The South African didn't speak either, no doubt feeling likewise. Bell was an unwanted presence and my hackles rose. Then I sharply told him to beat it, calling him a tactless swine. He went off, sniggering.

'God, some of these creatures are cheeky,' said the South African, to which I agreed wholeheartedly. He then introduced himself as Rory Ker, and we continued chatting until the master arrived a few minutes later.

He was a shortish, solidly built eighteen-year-old, with narrow blue eyes, and was soon picked for the First XV rugger team.

Me and the People at Eton

As the days went on I became very friendly with him and occasionally paid him a visit in his house, where he was in the Library. I don't recall any occasion that we talked about racialism, but in the English divisions he soon saw how I was racially abused by half the division and how I retaliated by hitting out. He didn't need to be told, therefore, that I was a very unpopular boy. He was usually very quiet and didn't talk much to the others. But a few boys took to him, and most respected and left him alone, for he was far older than anybody else and was only at Eton for that term. So he received the 'guest' treatment.

He always kept out of my problems and wanted no part of it. I understood, of course, that it would have been very awkward for him to put his nose in. A white South African helping a black man against racialism! Ironic, and joke of the week! And we would both undoubtedly become the centre of much ridicule, abuse and torment. Very embarrassing! And I felt he was right to have kept out of it. What he did do on some occasions when we walked off together after divisions was to tell me that I shouldn't retaliate physically as it would only antagonize and make matters worse for me. He used to condemn my tormentors as being very childish. I used to say that I'd try to ignore my tormentors, but that it was difficult. I knew of course that I would find it difficult not to resort to brute force. However, I respected him enough not to lose my temper if he happened to be present in an abusive company, as was occasionally the case, and our friendship always remained intact.

Sometime around the middle of term he and the other South African invited me to tea one evening. We had it in The Century, one of the two oldest restaurants on the High Street over 500 years old. The other South African's name was Paul Shapiro, a dark boy as old but bigger than Ker, who also played in the First XV and spoke with the same sort of accent. I rarely saw him in the school, and when I did, usually in the streets or doing physical training in the gym, we always exchanged greetings and talked for some moments. He, Ker and I sat down to a meal of scrambled eggs on toast, during which we mostly discussed the school. At the end of the meal, I pulled out my wallet with the intention of paying for my share. But Shapiro stopped me with a smile, saying that as they had invited me to the meal, I couldn't pay. After protesting, I put my wallet back and silently watched them arguing amicably about who was going to pay how much. Neither of them could have guessed what was on my mind. I was in a sea of deep thought about apartheid, and with deep solemnity I was wondering: Is it really based on some sacred truth? Is it possible that a black man does not automatically contaminate the whites? Is it possible that white South Africans are not necessarily damned by eating at the same table as a black man? Could the stiffnecks of the Dutch Reformed Church have perhaps got hold of the wrong God? . . . I wondered also why I had had more common decency shown to me by these two South Africans than by almost any other white boy at Eton. It made me feel deeply sorry for the South African system and all who live under it, black and white alike.

Because Ker and Shapiro were so decent to me, I was contented to believe they were anti-apartheid, and I don't recall having ever thought of asking them their feelings on the matter. It never occurred to me that they could have supported it to the hilt and all the good friendship they showed me was just put on to hide their guilt. I have been tempted to believe that this might well have been the case, but you can never tell – it might not have been. The fact remains that they were good to me and my feeling of gratitude and respect for them will never change.

The only time I ever mentioned apartheid to any of them was when the row about South Africa and the Mexico Olympics erupted. In the division room one morning I approached Ker at his desk and expressed my thought that the countries who opposed South Africa's entry were being puerile; after all the Games had nothing to do with politics.

'Well, I suppose you're right, Dillibe,' he replied, 'but those are just problems that we have to face.'

'That's true,' I agreed. 'I think I'll write a letter to one of the national papers and express my views.'

And I did in fact write to the *Daily Telegraph* and the letter was published. I told them exactly the same thing as I told Ker, and said that South Africa was being fair in sending a mixed team and she should be allowed to take part. I added that I was a West African Negro. All sorts of letters poured in to me about it, and from many masters and boys I received congratulations for having achieved the correspondence columns of the *Daily Telegraph*! The *Eton College Chronicle* offered me their journalistic congratulations. And inside my house, I had a lot of arguments about it. But I knew that the only reason the letter was published was because an African Negro wrote it, thus disagreeing with what the black African countries were complaining about: not because it was a brilliant work of art or anything like that.

Quietly I showed Ker a cutting of the letter in the division, and he rather liked it. But little did he or anybody else suspect that I had deluded them as to what were my true feelings about the whole situation, and was mocking their ignorance. The truth was that I was sincerely hoping that the white South Africans would be defeated and humbled by black athletes, and curse their luck for ever having put themselves to such a test.

'Say, Harry, will you sock me?!' . . . 'Sure! What would you like?!' . . . 'Sorry, I can't afford it.' In noisy Rowland's and other tuck shops, those were the most common questions one would hear. I was a frequent user of those questions: I asked boys to sock me many more times than I used to be asked, and I was socked more times than I socked others.

No, I didn't always meet with hostility and hatred. Throughout my time at the school there were a good number of friendly and decent boys. From time to time I found difficulty with my set work, for example, and the helping hands of boys in my block, and above, were always there when I entered their rooms in the evenings with my difficulties. After I became a Specialist I often pestered boys in my house who owned record players to play me my favourite tracks, and they nearly always did so. I used to be aware of boys' kind actions and was really grateful for them, but I regret that I was more conscious and embittered at all the racial prejudice. However, apart from the kind actions, I did also have some friends. There were quite a number of boys who were always friendly because they admired my big, black figure and my prowess at games to go with it: some of them often savagely turned on their allies when they racially abused me, and I used to feel a sense of respect for them. Finally there were about half a dozen boys in mine and other houses whose rooms I was constantly visiting. They were very much in my favour, and showed a liberal attitude to my ways of dealing with racial abuse, and always remained very friendly towards me. But when I got into my conflicts they kept right out, and let me do as I saw fit. Though they had an open mind to the whole thing, they would have preferred that I didn't use violence and just ignored all the abuse. This is what they would have done, they told me.

Yes, I did have friends at Eton. But speaking honestly, I did not have what one can call a *true* friend: a good friend in whose company I was always in, say; a steady, trustworthy friend. Somebody as friendly as mess mates were. All the friendship shown to me by any boy was really superficial. I have to admit that I could have made some very good friends but for my violent manner. Despite the medieval advice of a few boys like, 'If you bloody smash them really hard, they wouldn't go on being so nasty to you', nearly everybody I knew always advised me to ignore the abuse and not take it to heart.

I would really have preferred to have had some good friends, and I was always aware that not many boys really liked me. However, I just accepted it as it was, and it didn't really bother me too much. But as I snuggled up in my bed at night, I often gave the whole thing long and sincere thought, and I could never agree to ignore the abuse and try and make friends. The reason was simply that I was an African, and the outlook of the average European and African towards provocation was different. The African, by nature, has always been very sensitive – much more sensitive than Europeans. If abused without provocation he will tend to fly out at his tormentor. But the European will ignore him or talk the whole thing out. The European deplores violence, and the African does not.

When I got into hot arguments with about half a dozen boys in a division room after I had hit or threatened to hit one of their friends whom they had prodded to molest me, I put this view forward several times. But not before I expressed, with irritation and boredom, that having known me long enough now, they must surely feel that it was rather childish to keep on, and still ask the same barbed questions about my race, designed to hurt me. Their counter was always that by hitting people, or threatening to, I was being childish myself, and until I learnt to take what was said to me without resorting to force, boys would continue their insults. Then I brought in the question of the difference in outlook between the Europeans and Africans.

'Well in Africa we use violence!' I used to shout challengingly, 'and I'm an African!'

'Well you're in England now!' came the quick counter. 'And while in England do as the English do!'

'If that's too difficult for you, then go back to wogland!' they added on more than one occasion.

I only regret that I didn't ask them why their colonial ancestors never did as the Africans when they came to Africa. Whether or not they had the whip over us, it was not their country! The point never occurred to me. However, the arguments used stubbornly to continue with none of us being satisfied. One point I recall I once put forward was if they ever stopped to think that *racial* abuse was wrong and was considered the extremest of all abuse by most people.

'This happens to be a free country,' they agreed, 'where one is entitled to free speech.'

'In which case I'm free to deal with your affronts in my own way!' I replied.

'Okay then, people'll just go on calling you names!' they said.

And so the questions did go on. 'How many maggots are there in your hair, Onyeama?' . . . 'Have you ever eaten human flesh?' . . . 'Is your father a witch doctor?' . . . 'Why are you black?' . . . 'What is it like being a wog?' . . . I nearly always exploded, and with sudden savagery jumped up from my seat or wherever I was standing, and scored with a heavy punch to the face or the stomach or on the arm of the boy before he could get away. The punches to the face and stomach made a few of them cry. Their smouldering friends would go into an orgy of racial abuse, shouted with the utmost hatred and bitterness. The attentions of the other boys present would be drawn and most of them would join in and jeer.

'You filthy wog, Onyeama! Dirty black nigger! We hate you – we hate all wogs! Everybody hates you here, so why not go back to the filth where you belong! You black thug! You're the only black one here, Onyeama, so fucking well watch it! All you can do is hit people. You can never use words, can you?'

That was the kind of abuse I was usually faced with, and those incidents were abundant throughout my time at Eton. And amid all that a boy would occasionally creep up from behind me and quickly, with ape noises, stroke my hair roughly or knock off my books from my desk and run off before I could get him, much to the joy of the others. They would be further delighted when he stood at a distance away, laughing and jumping up and down like an ape, holding his armpits. The feeling of bitterness was very mutual, and I always shouted back racial abuse of my own. They looked very threatening, and I was afraid that a combined attack would be launched. With my heart skipping frantically, I was ready to fight for my life. But they never attacked, and I have often wondered if perhaps they feared that because of my size and race they would meet with tough opposition. I have liked to think that was the case. What usually happened was that a full-scale racialist row between us would break out again, and violence. It was usually the rapid entry of a few boys who had been mobbing outside that sent everybody scurrying off to their seats, much to my intense relief. The master was coming.

So that was how the situation stood, and I regret very much that I was not popular as a person. But I have always liked to think that I was in the right. And another reason I felt, and still feel now, that I could not have ignored the insults is that it would mean being an Uncle Tom's Nigger. It would be just cowardly, putting myself at my abusers' mercy, at their own request and letting them have their own way. I should take all the abuse offered me just because they preferred it that way!

Just as it is ironical that two of the most friendly boys I met at Eton were the South Africans, the same can be said when I recall that one of my enemies, believe it or not, was my fellow black boy at the school, Tokunbo Akintola. It would seem that I have a knack for making friends and enemies with the wrong people!

Akintola was the son of the Western Nigerian Prime Minister, Chief Samuel Akintola. For being the first African at Eton, he became world famous. I first knew of him when I was still at my prep school and I read in the papers, that Lent term of 1964, that the first African boy ever had passed the Common Entrance examination into Eton. I have to admit honestly that I was immediately terribly jealous, since I myself had been the first to have my name put down for the school. I knew this because my housemaster told my prep school Headmaster when I was brought for an interview in summer 1963. But now I was going to arrive second, simply because I failed the entrance exam and Akintola passed. I had only myself to blame.

Be that as it may, I retained my jealousy for several weeks after I first met Akintola in Judy's Passage my first day at the school. Thereafter for that term, I completely ignored him when we passed in the streets, and he did the same. Quite often I was asked by boys in divisions and in my house what I thought of him, and I generally avoided a straight answer by replying that I did not know him well enough to pass any opinions. My evasiveness did not go unnoticed, and it was during my second term that a rumour started that my family and his had a blood feud. For three days I was approached all over the school, even by boys I did not know at all, and asked if this was true. I always emphatically denied it, and tried my best to find out how the story had started. My father had been a friend of Chief Akintola for over twenty years, and it was a little mystifying.

Eventually I found out that a boy in my house whom I shall call Michael had noticed the cool manner between Akintola and myself and deduced erroneously that there was a feud on between our families. Michael was a tall, plump boy with long brown hair parted in the middle. I had never really taken to him. He was argumentative and had a very nasty temper. One afternoon I went to his very tidy room as he was reading in his armchair, and sharply asked what right he had in spreading this rumour, threatening to go to my housemaster and report him. He ducked the questions and tried to farm the blame on Akintola, saying that the story had originally come from him. I made it quite clear that it was totally untrue and very embarrassing, and he should refrain from spreading it if he wanted no trouble. At least he agreed politely and apologized. And I decided that I would not allow the matter to rest until I had tackled Akintola about it, and put a final halt to the rumour. The next time I saw him was late on a Sunday afternoon, two days later. I met him on the steps of School Hall as he was on his way down the High Street, and angrily demanded an explanation. He listened quite expressionlessly and then calmly replied, 'Michael told me that it was you who started the story.' He was totally unmoved and uninterested, and without another word, nonchalantly stalked off down the street, hands in pockets.

I allowed the matter to drop, and thinking about it later, I began to realize the puerility of my jealousy and refusal to get on with Akintola. One afternoon I saw him sitting in Rowland's eating potato crisps and reading a comic, and I saw it as a good opportunity to start making the peace. I went and sat opposite him and greeted him by his nickname Toks. Once more he just looked at me without any expression of pleasure or otherwise, and returned the greeting flatly. We started to talk rather stiffly about the school, and he said he disliked it much more through boredom than anything else, although he had only been there for two terms.

From then on, we talked to each other in the streets whenever we met, and I began to hope we were friends. His room was a small, scantily decorated one and occasionally I visited him there. He never came round to mine – or even, for that matter, to my house.

Then things began to change. One hot afternoon in the summer of 1965, I was quietly looking out of the window in a noisy mathematics division room when a big, very handsome boy called Bethel approached me. He was a quiet, clever fellow whom I liked. He approached me smiling and asked what I thought of Akintola. By this time, of course, I had changed from my rather evasive attitude and replied cheerfully that I liked him.

Bethel frowned. 'You do?' he replied.

'Yes, why, don't you or something?' I answered.

'Yes, I like him, he's a great fellow; but I'm surprised you do.'

'Why?'

'Well, he didn't seem to like you very much when I spoke to him the other day.'

'What did he say?' I asked, rather surprised to hear this.

'Well I asked him what he thought of you, and he said "I try not to".'

Bethel said all this in a very simple and truthful way, and I had no reason to suspect that he was lying. I was not hurt but simply surprised that Akintola should have said it when I thought we had become firm friends. Matters then reverted to the old format of totally ignoring each other. Occasionally I went and spoke to him in the tuck shops, but his replies were pretty curt and not really like those of a friend. I started to wonder what the hell I could have done, and it took a few days before I recalled my first few weeks at Eton, during the time when I was jealous of Akintola. I have to admit that I used to say some unkind things about his father to boys in my house. They would ask me whether he was a good politician, and I always said no. I knew really very little about him as a politician and just said no out of spite to satisfy my jealousy for Akintola. I always referred to his father as 'scarface', because of the number of deep tribal scars he had.

Akintola and I barely ever spoke to each other again until after the Christmas holidays of 1965, which was when tragedy struck his family. I was down in Oxfordshire staying with my guardian when I heard the news of a military *coup* in Nigeria. Many civilians and in particular politicians were murdered, and among them was Chief Akintola. I was naturally very shocked to hear the news, but there was worse to come when I got back to school for the Lent term.

On the first night of term, my housemaster came in to see me as I finished unpacking my suitcase. After a brief conversation about how the holidays had gone and what I had done, he suddenly said, 'I'm very sorry to hear about Akintola.'

'Yes, Chief Akintola,' I replied gravely, 'it was tragic.'

'No, no, not Chief Akintola, I know about him. I mean the son – the one who is here. We heard on the wireless this morning that he had been shot.'

My face crumpled and I swallowed violently. A strange sensation of fire coursed through my body, making my skin tingle. The news burnt a hole in my brain.

'Him?!' I replied with stunned disbelief. 'No!'

'Yes, I'm afraid so,' he replied sadly.

'Sh—Sh—Shot dead?!'

'No, no, not dead. They say he was wounded in the leg.'

A great tide of relief surged into my heart, but I was still very much shaken by the news. We discussed Akintola for a few more minutes and then said goodnight.

Understandably there was a good deal of excitement about it in my house when I told the news in the morning. Boys expressed their sympathy, saying how lucky I was that I was not in Nigeria, and that my father was not a politician. The whole thing became the centre of much talk in the school, and many boys approached me about it.

Then the story started to change. The news that came from the trouble-torn Nigeria left a grey cloud of concern and uncertainty gripping the whole school. One day the reports said that *only* Chief Akintola was killed, another day that *all* the members of his family present in the house as well, and, finally, *certain* members of his family. The days dragged along into weeks, and no news about Akintola came. The whole school was thus forced into the grim belief that he was dead. A brief article appeared in the gossip column of the *Sunday Express* reporting his absence from Eton and the belief that he was dead. And I understood that a special prayer was said for him in both chapels one morning. I wrote a letter to my father later that day asking what he knew. His reply was prompt: Akintola was alive and well, but was unlikely to come back to Eton for a while because of all that he and his mother had been through. I informed a lot of boys of this great news and of course there was much relief.

It was four weeks after the term began that Akintola eventually returned. After evening Chapel one Sunday, Michael excitedly rushed into my room and told me that Akintola was back. He said that Akintola had been in Chapel and looked very sorry for himself, but appeared to be quite unscathed. Of course I was delighted to hear this, and was very eager to see Akintola and hear exactly what had happened. My opportunity came in the afternoon the next day. I met him by chance in Alden and Blackwell, one of the school's stationers on the High Street. He was just putting back a book on its shelf when I approached him and cheerfully greeted him. Then my smile froze! Before I could say anything more, he shortly returned my greeting, turned and left the shop. There were a number of other boys there, presenting their book lists signed by their housemasters, and looking at books. But thank goodness nobody noticed this rebuff: it would have been extremely embarrassing if they had. I left several seconds later, feeling a bit hurt. Oh, my God, I thought, back to square one!

Throughout that term, we did not exchange a single word. The only person I recall mentioning this tense relationship to was my dame when she came to see me one night, and asked how Akintola was getting on. And after telling her, I added positively that I had no idea why the situation was like this. She was rather taken aback and didn't really know what to say except that it was rather strange, and she wondered why. She in turn passed my information on to my housemaster who, in the dining-room after lunch (a few days later) announced that he wanted to see me. He saw me last in the queue outside his study and suggested that the best thing I could do was to keep away from Akintola. He gave me a very likely reason why Akintola had been so unpleasant: it was one that had never occurred to me – that Akintola's father and relatives had been killed by Ibo soldiers, and I myself am an Ibo. I felt that my housemaster's suggestion was good and I kept away from him as much as possible, also thinking it the most tactful thing to do.

Then came the school play *Caesar and Cleopatra*. This was another occasion I had to speak with him, and it became increasingly difficult. We both got parts as Nubian sentinels, and my part being quite a bit bigger than his, I tried to help him with advice. But he stubbornly refused to be advised and on many occasions we broke into hot arguments in the dressing-room. Nobody's attention, as far as I was aware, was ever drawn to this, probably because they were all pretty noisy themselves. Thereafter things never improved, and that was really how life between Akintola and myself continued for the rest of our time at Eton.

He spoke English brilliantly – much better than I did – with a slow accent just like an Englishman. I'm afraid, however, that he wasn't able to offer anything that could change the Etonian outlook towards the Africans. I learnt from boys in his divisions that he was not good at work and was usually low in his fortnightly positions. He didn't take much interest in games, and I only knew him to be a rower. I learnt that two of his greatest interests were fashion and pop music.

I never actually saw him racially abused, and I don't recall any occasion when he saw me victimized. When we were on speaking terms, we never mentioned anything about colour problems in the school. But I reckoned that he must surely know about my unpopularity. He was undoubtedly more skilled in handling racial abuse than I was, using the simple technique of ignoring remarks thrown at him. In division rooms when I was jeered at, he was often mentioned. 'Akintola doesn't go around hitting everybody!' my tormentors shouted. 'So why should you?' And my reply was always that we both have different characters. And so since he never used violence, he enjoyed a very much quieter life than I did. A good number of people expressed a dislike for him, and their reasons were that he talked too much and was very conceited and always showed off about his family's wealth and position.

On the whole, though, Akintola was popular at Eton (certainly very much more popular than I was) for two reasons: he was considered desperately cool because of the most elegant clothes he often wore, and he was often socking boys in the tuck shops. He was obviously one of those Africans who are not really bothered by people's words, and I was one of those who are. In the Summer term of 1966, he left for another school in Geneva after passing two 'O' levels out of four. All over the school I came across a lot of boys who were sorry that he was going, and in my division rooms, my enemies deeply expressed their wish that I would leave instead. My feelings were mixed: I knew I would not miss him as a friend, but it was very comforting to have another Negro at Eton.

*

One of the reasons for Eton's fame is that many sons of prominent and wealthy citizens go there, and members of the aristocracy. There was quite a number of them when I was there, but only about half a dozen whom I knew personally. Only a few of them showed any visible signs of snobbery. Without their having to say anything, you would wonder who the hell does this chap think he is to carry such an air of self-importance about him. Several of such characters were discussed in boys' rooms now and again. One, for example, was Lord Andrew Burgersh, son of the Earl of Westmoreland. A small, dark boy with a freckled face well over a year younger than I was. Good at games, and lousy at work, he was one of those in my block who left the school after failing to get enough 'O' levels. He was a very proud character, and one could see his pride in the rather happy, self-conscious manner in which he normally walked, with hands in his pockets. For my first year, he and I loathed each other's guts. It was this abuse-and-violence problem, and we were often conflicting. But eventually we managed to become more friendly. We attended the same divisions, and it was mostly there that one could detect the snobbery in him. He was a rough character, a loud-mouth, and was normally the chief and frequent orator, especially in the riotous mobbings. 'Attention please!!! LORD Burgersh speaking!' That was the atmosphere about him all the time.

An amusing incident that involved him occurred in Mr Chamier's mathematics division one morning. While he was explaining at the board, Lord Burgersh and another boy were angrily exchanging punches in the back row. The boy was Sir William Jaffray, a rough fellow of medium size with unkempt hair, whom boys found childish. It so happened that Mr Chamier turned and caught them at it.

'Right!', he bellowed angrily, and walked over to his desk to mark their names down. 'That books Jaffray's and Burgersh's seats for Saturday! You will both come in here on fourth school Saturday (for most divisions, there was no fourth school on Saturdays, and the boys were free until lunch) and do some maths. Then you can fight to your heart's content!' Next he sternly addressed the division. 'So remember! Anybody else who feels like irritating me will come in here on Saturday and have a free seat for this gruelling battle for the throne between his Lordship and Sir William!'

Typical Mr Chamier wit indeed! And everybody bellowed with laughter. I always felt very snobbish myself at Eton actually, because, being black, I was aware that just about the whole school knew me. I reckoned that everybody must have seen my name in the *Eton College Alphabetical List*, who my father was and his address. Until early 1967, my father had been put down as the Honourable Mr Justice Onyeama, Federal Supreme Court, Lagos, Nigeria. I felt yet more proud and snobbish when he became appointed to the International Court of Justice, in the Hague, and was therefore addressed as His Excellency Judge Onyeama. Not only that, but also that he was a member of the world's highest court. And I felt only too happy to talk about it when boys and masters occasionally flattered me that I was lucky to have a father in such an important position, asked about the International Court and what kind of cases were held there.

Where I felt snobbish most of all was in the streets. I was always aware of the stares I received from the public and passing vehicles, and I used to adore it; especially in the summer, when tourists flocked in at the weekends to sight-see, and used to point at me as I walked past. The same applied to those in coaches, who often took quick camera shots of me. I always felt valuable when I was approached by tourists and asked to pose for a photo. Nearly always I politely refused, simply because I would have felt embarrassed standing there. A few times when I was in the company of one or two boys, I agreed to be photographed with them.

Where I enjoyed the stares most of all was in Windsor, because it was more populated than Eton. I often went there, usually alone, and mostly on Saturdays. I always went to WHSmith's, the bookshop, to look at magazines and listen to records. Though we were allowed up to the Castle, I never went, as I had no interest in sight-seeing or historic buildings. I chose Saturdays particularly to go to Smith's, because the shop and the streets were more crowded with tourists and shoppers, which meant more stares. Yes, in public I was arrogant and proud to be a black Etonian! I must admit that that was partly why I enjoyed going up to Windsor. And inside Smith's, my mind was just as intent on the staring faces as on the magazines and records.

It was, I imagined, out of sheer curiosity and interest that I was mostly stared at. But on a number of occasions, I did come across hostile looks, and ones of scorn and seemingly disgust. This applied to members of the public and a few shopkeepers when I entered their shops. My immediate feelings were that they were colour prejudiced. In their minds were branded bad ideas of the dark continent – Africa: the jungle – the place where the blacks lived primitively with animals and practised their dark and half-forgotten secrets – witchcraft. And here, astonishingly enough, I was – at ETON, wearing a tail-coat! It was like a monkey wearing a tail-coat: in other words, somebody who shouldn't be where he is. Those were their thoughts, I felt sure: they were also undoubtedly angry and envious, I felt, much to my amusement.

I found that most of the shopkeepers in Eton showed me a lot of respect and kindness: more, I felt, than the average Etonian. Most of them could never miss greeting me heartily when I entered their shops and asking what I had been up to. I used to think that they admired me, especially as some of them used to inquire with interest how I was improving with certain games. I was tempted to believe that the reason they particularly respected me was because they probably felt that for me to be in a community like this, I must be exceptionally bright and son of an important or *wealthy* father – all rather unusual for an African.

It was the kindness shown to me in the independent shop called Tudor Stores that I have always remembered. It was a food shop a little further down the High Street from Rowland's, and was owned by the Speller family, a very cheerful couple with a pretty, six foot daughter in her early twenties. Theirs was a three-roomed shop: there was the main public one, and two inner ones used only by the boys to read comics and eat light grills. They were always cheerful and ultra-kind to me: they often used to give me drinks and sweets free, their reasons always being 'You're so far away from home, Ony!' Only on one or two occasions do I vaguely recall them doing this for an ordinary Etonian. However, I was never aware of any envy amongst the other boys present because of their extra kindness towards me. I recall that on my first Fourth of June, after my guardian and his wife had gone home late in the afternoon, I and another dark-haired fellow in my block, whom I hardly knew, were the only customers present in Tudor Stores. We were both invited by Mrs Speller to have supper with the family after they closed at six o'clock. And on two more occasions during my time they invited me to tea on Sundays.

Much as I felt proud to walk the streets in my uniform, I still, at heart, did not think much of it as a school uniform. My feelings from when I first put it on never changed, and the occasions did come when I felt very embarrassed to wear it. Those occasions were mostly during Summer terms in the sunny evenings. I would be nonchalantly walking up or down the High Street with the creatures of science and nature, when I am suddenly met with a torrent of racial abuse screamed so loudly and so unexpectedly by many voices that I almost jump out of my skin. 'Black cunt! Go back to the jungle! Darkie! Nigger boy! . . . Bongo Bongo, get back to the Congo!', etc., with mocking laughter to accompany them. My abusers this time were not Etonians, but long-haired Teddy-boys packed in garish, painted cars and motorcycles noisily thundering past. For a stunned second I stumbled back in somewhat the fearful ecstasy of a dog coming upon his first jumping toad. Usually by the time I realized what was happening, they were halfway down the street waving back 'V'-signs. The embarrassment was so humiliating that I felt my hair trying hard to uncurl and stand on end. I felt like a side of beef on a hook in a slaughter-house as I was invaded by faces of Etonians and members of the public. I would try to hide my embarrassment by sighing with exaggerated triviality and walking on grinning, but I was cursing bitterly under my breath, hot fever throbbing within my veins.

There used to be little reaction from the passers-by whenever this happened. Who could tell what feelings or expressions they held? I deliberately avoided their faces. But I always liked to imagine that they were disapproving and sympathetic. I recall that on a few of the numerous occasions that this happened, there were sighs of disgust from a few Etonian boys, who roared back foul-mouthed abuse at the speeding cars accompanied with 'V'-signs. I felt this was done out of sympathy and to ease off any bitter feelings that might have been left in me. Admittedly I did find them pretty comforting, but I took little notice of them.

I was hurt, not so much by the abuse itself, but more by the embarrassing stares I received. I truly did wish that there was some way I could disappear. I knew positively that the school uniform was mostly to blame: I was so conspicuous in it. The abuse always came when I was wearing it, and *never* when I was in change. The reason was quite simple: in change I looked like a common nigger, and nobody, unless of course they knew me, would guess that I was an Etonian – but it was rare to see a nigger at Eton wearing a tail-coat and striped trousers. So if I reckoned I was high and mighty, the youths probably thought, they had better let me know that they reckoned otherwise.

However, Etonians, I understood, were not popular with these Teddy-boy types: or shall I say the underprivileged youths. Now and again rumours used to circulate the school about Etonians being attacked and beaten up by them. It was undoubtedly the snobbish uniform that was much of the cause for this. Obviously inside these youths lurked deep envy and inferiority complexes.

That being the case, they were, at least, more privileged characters as far as wooing girls was concerned; for they had no restrictions on their movements, nor were they under the taboos of aristocratic behaviour which the Etonians had to comply with. The end result was that the Etonians seldom, if ever, had girls to talk with, let alone have an affair with. They found that they had to stick to a unisexual atmosphere, which led some of them to situations that radically transformed their behaviour.

I never really gave thought to girls at Eton: they just never came into my mind. But I enjoyed sitting in rooms and listening with interest to boys' tittle-tattle about their sexual exploits in the holidays, and the beauty of the familiar girls that lived or worked in Eton, like housemasters' daughters and shop assistants. I never put in any words, because I had no sexual exploits to relate, and I had never really considered the beauty of any of the girls in Eton. I regarded them as human beings more than beautiful bodies, and took little notice of them. But I must admit that there were occasions that fancy thoughts did flash across my mind that some of them may have an admiration and liking for my big, black figure. When I met them in shops and in the streets and we exchanged smiles of recognition, I used to enjoy imagining that. Of course, I never found out if that was the case, and so never enjoyed anything more than my fantasies.

There was no doubt that it was very few of the pretty girls who walked through Eton that missed the notice and unblinking stares of Eton boys. I occasionally used to be in a company of boys that pricked their ears and muttered gasps of pleasure at a beautiful one approaching, and helplessly passed comments to each other. An example was one fine Sunday afternoon in my second year. With ease, two boys in my block and myself aimlessly strolled down the High Street when a mini-skirted blonde approached on the opposite pavement. She was well-built and walked with a wiggle which made my friends' mouths water. They crossed over at once, muttering gasps and talking 'dirty'. And as the young girl passed us some moments later, one of my friends, a very daring ruffian with red, curly hair, loudly and deliberately said to the other boy, 'Say, Bill, mini-skirts should be rolled up twelve inches higher!' The girl, of course, heard the comment but just continued on her way, leaving us in a very amused state.

There was an atmosphere of sex at Eton all the time. The only kind of sex that occurred or was usually talked about was that between males – homosexuality!

Chapter Seven
Homosexuality

Although there was an atmosphere of sex all the time in the school, the only type that took place or was usually talked about was homosexuality.

This practice was not uncommon in the unisexual status of the school; the only scandal was getting caught. A number of boys were caught and flogged; four were expelled for homosexual assault in the form of buggery. At the end of the day, one was only surprised that it was not a Conservative government, with so many Old Etonians in it, to amend the laws on homosexuality.

It is a striking fact that not until some four weeks into my career at Eton did I discover the meaning of the words 'homosexual' and 'queer', and that both had the same definition. I heard their frequent usage in my short time at the school, and was aware that they applied to all sorts of boys, but their precise meaning was what I did not immediately realize. It was an eye-opener when I learnt that homosexuality was common practice in Britain. Back home in Nigeria, and at my preparatory school, boys had been attracted sexually to each other, but, in retrospect, I saw it as a passing phase for all children.

In my innocence, I could not have dreamt that my own

involvement in 'mobbing' (forbidden horseplay) – a commonplace among Etonians – would single me out for a charge of
homosexual tendencies . . . precisely because I was black. A char-
acteristically Nigerian habit which had not abandoned me in the
process of change in England was the wholly innocuous and well-
meaning friendly gesture of putting my arms around boys'
shoulders and necks. It was appreciated at Grove Park Preparatory School, and there were no suggestions of a sexual advance
or any expressed revulsion of such close physical contact. But at
Eton it was deplored with such outcries as, 'Take your bloody arms
off me, you fucking queer!' and 'We don't do that sort of thing in
this country, Onyeama!' In classrooms, it drew the attention of
almost everybody, triggering off a spate of ape-mimicry and racial
slurs. 'He wants to go to bed with you!' they would tease the blushing victims of my touch. At the swimming pool, it was common
to see boys pushing each other in, although it was not allowed. I
would take them in with a flying tackle instead, landing in the
water with my arms around them. There would be expressed
amazement from many onlookers and the usual racial slurs, 'Black
queer. Filthy homo. You're not in bloody wogland now.'

On another occasion in a boy's room in my house, it almost
brought me trouble. About five of us were chatting, and presently
the conversation became noisy, turning ultimately into a free-for-
all horseplay. I went for a handsome, fair-haired chap called
Timothy Elliot, and held him in a tight bear-hug, with my arms
clenched tightly around his back. There was an explosion of
astonishment from everybody, halted in their tracks by the spectacle of my close physical contact with Elliot. 'Christ, Onyeama,

are you in love with him?' one boy shouted. 'And look,' screamed another, 'Elliot's flies are undone. Scandal. Bloody scandal.'

Hearing all this, Elliot, who had been trying vainly to break free, lost his cool and shouted, 'Yes go on let go, you dirty queer. Let me go.' I released him and he retired, blushing furiously, to the ottoman on the other side of the room, and sat down. He hid his face behind a newspaper. 'That's bloody bad, Onyeama,' I was told, 'you shouldn't do a thing like that; it's filthy.'

'What's filthy about it?' I wanted to know; 'After all, wrestlers do it on television.'

At that moment the door swung open, and a member of The Library called Jimmy Fletcher stood there, trying unsuccessfully to conceal a smile. He was tall and thin, with long, ragged hair, and was one of the more affable members of The Library – much favoured by the 'lower' boys.

'What's going on in here?' he asked, looking round the room. 'We were just having fun,' he was told.

'Yes, I know; I heard all your fun. Just keep the bloody noise down, and don't let me have to come in here again. If I do you'll all be heavily fined.' He turned towards the door, and a smile came over his face again. 'And all this I hear about flies being undone . . .'

'That was a joke,' he was assured.

'Well, let's have no more jokes like that,' he said, and left the room.

As soon as he was gone, we all fell about laughing. Fletcher's smile had indicated that no serious action would be taken, and I was relieved to have avoided a beating, for another member of The Library might have thought it not so funny.

The significant issue about that incident was Elliot's reaction to my hug – the vehemence with which he finally rebelled. I was thinking that it had something to do with the widespread revulsion of being accused (albeit playfully) of indulging in a sexual act with an African. The only difference in his case was that he did not deliver himself of the usual racial slur that accompanied the outrage of the other boys whom I played with in the same manner.

At the end of the day I was obliged to desist from mobbing with my schoolmates in the wake of a little tussle I had with a boy in my house. I got the upper hand, sat on him, and pinned his hands victoriously together over his head. He came on with the 'queer' hysteria as he shouted that I should get off him. When I complied, he got to his feet and mouthed every imaginable charge of homosexual inclinations on my part. The incident circulated the school like bushfire, and brought me too much attention from amused friends and foes wanting to know if it was true. When I insisted that it had been an innocuous friendly tussle, I was told, 'You don't go having friendly fights with small boys or anyone else, Onyeama. It sounds suspicious, mighty suspicious.'

For sure I did not deserve such false slander.

There was, however, an ironic twist to the end of the accusations of homosexuality I received. Towards the end of my career at the school, a friend of mine in my house (whom I shall call 'Nick') developed an occasional fondness for visiting my room after 'lock-up' to wrestle with me. He was a beefy rough-tough character with perpetually tousled brown hair and somewhat effeminate facial features, and eminently popular because of his witty, lively and carefree manner. There *might* have been a covert 'masochistic' flair in his enjoyment of being always overpowered and held down in our friendly tussles, after which he would collapse in my armchair and we would laugh and tittle-tattle. Once we discussed the subject of homosexuality, and I lamented over the false rumour tying me to the practice.

'I believe you that you are not a queer,' he said quietly. 'Nobody would agree to queer with you.'

'Why?' said I in genuine innocence.

'Because you are black,' he disclosed in a secretive tone, as if even the walls might hear this thunderbolt.

He needed to say no more. The point had been well entrenched.

Chapter Eight
Allowances

Away now from the sex-minded boys to a more respectable figure: a person whose only view of homosexuality, I gathered, was that big boys should not associate with little boys because of sexual attraction. A person who had something to accuse me of, but whose accusation was, at least, true and nothing like as embarrassing as the homosexual accusations: a person who treated me differently from the boys because of my colour. That person was my housemaster.

Oxford-educated, he was an Old Etonian himself, and had a number of daughters and a son, all, except one teenaged daughter, grown-up and unmarried. His son too was at Eton and later at Oxford, and had left the school two or three years before my time. He, my housemaster, was nicknamed 'Rubberneck' by the boys, because of the numerous deep wrinkles on his long, broad neck. Reputed to be the most boring chaplain and the most boring teacher the school had ever known, he seemed popular enough in my house, though it was generally felt he jumped to conclusions too quickly. To the boys, he was not very good-humoured: just serious and respectable, with normally a quiet and controlled temper. He gave up his housemastership a term before I left, after he'd served the traditional fifteen years. But he moved into a house in Eton and continued preaching and teaching for a few more terms before eventually retiring from the school.

His accusation against me took place on the very last night of his last term. He came into my room as I was combing my hair at the mirror after a nice hot bath. As usual, lips pursed in contemplation, hands stowed away in the light-blue trousers of his everyday clerical suit, he had a worried expression on his face. He spoke about my work and said that he was going to write to my father and suggest that I leave within the next year for a coaching establishment. With a firm, driving voice, he went on to say that when I got there I would seriously have to buck up and really concentrate on my work, that I was quite capable of passing the 'A' levels if I really tried, but he didn't think I really put enough seriousness into my work. Much as I knew that was true, I still protested mildly that I was trying. He persisted and added that I also had to learn to show some gratitude to the efforts people were making to help me. His voice was charged with feeling, and held a tinge of rebuke. Nervously, under his immobile, penetrating stare, I mumbled and was about to reply that I was grateful when he spoke again. 'You know, you've never come to thank me for what I've done for you! Over the years your father has often been writing to thank me, but *you have never once* thanked me!' His words came boldly and decisively. They fell heavily and I felt their impact and their chill. 'It's a very sad thing for me to have to say on my last night, Charles, but there it is,' he went on after a slight pause, turning for the door. 'However goodnight, and extend my best wishes to your family.'

'Goo—Goodnight, sir.' My throat almost jammed, my voice was more of a squeal.

As he went out, he delivered me a final glance full of sadness. I stood there frustrated and with a heavy heart, not knowing what to do or say. A barbed silence invaded the room. The joyful thoughts of the long, nine-week summer holidays vanished from my mind, and I stood there like a winter-bitten range bull dying by inches. It most certainly was a sad thing for my housemaster to have said on his last night, and as I thought about it, my whole body was stricken with distress and a guilty conscience. I knew that what he had said was true: I had never thanked him. As I will show soon, there were a number of things he did for me especially, and it was clearly obvious from his words that he meant he had expected me to know that he was doing them because I was different from everybody else by being black, and he felt particularly concerned about my welfare and happiness. I suspected that the matter had been on his mind for some time, and he had looked for a chance to tell me.

For a long time I restlessly walked about in my room among my packed baggage. I kept feeling like going out to him with sincere apologies and thanking him for all his help and kindness, but the courage was beyond me. I was also that sort of person who would feel too embarrassed to go and apologize to someone for something that I had done and admit my misdeed. Much as I knew how very hurt my housemaster was, all I could do was dejectedly allow the matter to pass – now, resolving firmly that I would certainly express my gratitude to him before I left the school.

I was always conscious of the things that my housemaster did for me in particular; conscious also that he obviously wanted to treat me more kindly and considerately than the other boys. It never did come into my mind that he might expect me to go and thank him for his great concern for me, but I was, genuinely, grateful inside – at least for most of the things he did, not all. The only thing I did not like was precisely the allowances he kept making for my continual bad work. Much as he showed a lot of concern about it and no doubt meant well, I found, as I have explained, the idea of his overlooking the great quantity of rips I was getting rather distasteful.

If *I* found that distasteful, so too did the boys in my house at other allowances he made for me. To give an example, I will begin by relating a conflict that I got into one lunch time during my second year. I was fifteen then, and was sitting at the bottom of the senior table. The second course of the meal was ice-cream and chocolate sauce. I did not favour it, and asked one of the Italian waiters to take it away. But the dame kicked up a fuss and insisted that I should eat something. She offered me the previous day's second course – bread and butter pudding, which I accepted gladly. It was soon brought, and as I tucked into it, the boy sitting opposite me, a witty, drowsy-looking fellow, drew several boys' attention to it.

'Why are you eating that filthy muck?' he asked in a lazy, somewhat flippant manner.

'Because I don't like ice-cream,' I answered logically.

'I suppose because it isn't black ice-cream,' he countered, looking away with a baleful glare.

The other boys looked at each other, trying unsuccessfully to hide amused faces. Nobody, except I, had anything to say to that. I was painfully embarrassed and I at once snarled at him to watch what he was saying, challenging him to meet me outside later on and to repeat it. His reply was an utterance of ape noises, and for some moments we exchanged racial abuse, with me issuing threats of violence later on and that I would complain to my housemaster. However, nothing further took place afterwards.

I would not have felt so hurt had I known that amid their silence, some of the other boys sympathized or supported me. But that was not the case. Because of my aggressive manner, none of them liked me at all. I knew that they were all for their friend, and I felt as if I was fighting against the lot of them, and so they were the target of my bitterness as well as their friend. Hardly any of them picked on me actually, it was normally their friend, though he didn't do it too often. I did, however, deliver him a powerful kick under the table now and again. The usual situation was that I was completely ignored – sent to Coventry. And this, to be honest, did not worry me much, for I normally liked to eat my meals without talking. And I knew it would be pointless my trying to engage in friendly conversations with anybody, because I was disliked and an unwanted presence. So I never tried.

The main reason for my unfortunate situation in this case was that according to my academic position in the house, I should not have been sitting at the senior table. I should, in fact, have been halfway up the junior table. The circumstances that saw me to the former occurred by my housemaster's feeling that I was too old to be sitting on the junior table.

It was in the Summer term of my second year that I moved up.

After breakfast on the first morning of term, the House Captain came round to my room to inform me of my housemaster's instructions, asking if that was all right with me. With concealed delight, I replied that it was fine. Truly, I was thrilled to hear this news. I used to feel so ashamed and humiliated to be the oldest of most of the junior table (from my second year, the very oldest), and sitting so low down, for I was always the most junior of the boys in my block. What's more I was bigger than everybody else, and this made me feel more out of place. And my conspicuousness added extra salt to the wound. I was so self-conscious about the whole matter, and it was partly the cause for my silence during meals. I was positive that the boys believed I was so low down because I was black and thus stupid.

Intense distaste and jealousy was shown by boys in my block and above at my moving up. During Chambers on the first day of term, I was in my room with my door open as they looked at the new seating arrangements for meals, which were marked on the noticeboards down the landing. Bitterly they expressed their distaste about my new place, and uttered obscene racial abuse. Amid the usual noises in the house, I could hear them very distinctly. They didn't know exactly why I had moved up, but they guessed, and guessed correctly; for, everybody in the house, just about, knew that I was rather old for my position in work. And one remark I clearly remember that the complainants agreed on was 'whose else's fault is it that he's so fucking thick?' There were about ten boys there, and their voices had the cold, ruthless quality of diamond slicing through glass. With an icy knot of uneasiness, I stood near the door and listened intently. For fear of being reviled, I was hesitating to go out until they had dispersed.

There were some boys in my block who didn't mind my moving up – those I usually got on with. When I went into their rooms they said, without any visible signs of envy, that it was because of my age. But I had no doubt that they had the feeling that it was fair in my case, for I had the wrong colour and race to be brainy enough to work my way higher up the table.

However, most of the boys in my block minded my moving up, and for a long time stopped talking to me; the same applied to most of the boys on the lower half of the senior table. They were between three to six terms senior to me, and obviously felt that I was too junior at work to be with them, whether I was their age or not, and it was wrongful to those senior to me who had to remain on the junior table (all but one). Though I did not much mind being sent to Coventry on the senior table, I did find the hostile attitude of the boys a bit discomforting. I have always been convinced that had I not been a violent character, most of the boys wouldn't have minded so much, if at all.

I started to sense that many boys in the house were now getting a bit fed up that my housemaster was making allowances for me. They knew about the profusion of rips I was getting and my housemaster's obvious intention not to put me on white ticket. And now this queue barging! Okay I'm black! So damned what? If I come to Eton, I'm an Etonian! Can't I be treated like everybody else? Aren't I still a human being? Am I *so* different that allowances must be made? If I'm going to make things awkward because I'm black, why the hell be allowed to remain in the school? . . . Those were my own ideas of what boys were thinking and saying. I could strongly feel it, and I could also read it in their baleful glances at me. And I must say, I felt that their points were very valid. I felt also that the boys had every right to complain about my moving up, as it was, really, unfair to them. But I was prepared to face all their hostility and complaints rather than remain so low down the junior table, and I felt very grateful to my housemaster for his consideration. I don't recall thinking this at the time, but I believe that the reason for his moving me up was deeper than my being too old. I clearly remember that I used to often look up to see him quietly staring at me in a nondescript sort of way. I thought nothing of it at all, but now I suspect strongly that he was observing my silence and pondering on the reasons for it. When I put myself in his position, I tend to believe that he was able to search my mind and conclude correctly that I was feeling embarrassed and out of place to be sitting so low down the table: not just that, but also to guess correctly at some of the reasons I have given for feeling so – size and age. And he obviously felt very sympathetic and decided to move me up. I am convinced that he would have kept me there had I seemed happy and talkative.

Another thing I never gave thought to at the time was if he would have done the same thing for a white boy of my size and age. In retrospect I am inclined to believe that he would not have done. He wouldn't have cared as much, I fancy, or been so sympathetic towards a white boy as he was to me, because, as I believed, he wanted to give me the 'guest' treatment owing to my being different from everybody else. Being particularly concerned about my happiness, as I felt he was, seemed the reason why he should keep looking at me during lunch. I fancy he would have found it a more difficult choice on whether or not to move up a white boy. He would have had to seriously consider whether, despite his age, it would be fair on the more senior boys. After all, it was entirely the boy's own fault that he was bad at work and thus so low down the table, and there was no excuse. But I, being an African, my case was different. I believe that ideas along those lines did swim in my housemaster's mind.

The jealousy that boys showed about my moving up took four terms to cool down. Then it was antagonized again, twice as fiercely, when halfway through the Michaelmas term of 1967 another major allowance was made for me: I was elected into Debate.

Now, to elect a boy into Debate, the members of the two house authorities met inside the Library at ten-thirty in the evening, where they discussed whom to elect and the responsibility of the boy. There were usually two elections a term, and up to three boys could be elected on the same night. Similar was an election into the Library, except that only Library members decided whom to elect. And after they had made up their minds as to whom, they would next quake the entire house to its foundation by thundering, at a run, up and down the landings like stampeding cattle, bellowing 'horray' at the top of their voices and hammering on boys' doors as they passed. This clamorous affair was traditional, and was merely done to announce to everybody that there was to be another disciplinary body in the house. After about four minutes, they would pound on the boy's door and pour in noisily, shouting congratulations and present him with the rules of the

House Library or Debating Society. In some houses, it was the thing to forcefully take off his clothes and pour cold water over him, and fling his things about – all done as a celebration. But in my house, it wasn't as rough as that.

I was awake dreaming in my bed when I was elected, and I can't truly say what a delightful surprise it was. When the Library and Debate swept into my room, switched on the light, swarmed over to my bed and shook my hand in turn, and presented me with the Debate rules, my eyes nearly bolted from my head and I almost gulped down my tongue with total incredulity! As the House Captain stood there holding out the Debate rules to me, I stared at him in amazement as if he'd gone raving mad: as if he needed to mend a few electric wires which must have fused in his brain. Much as I expressed astonishment, I was able, in my exult-ation, to realize that it might be a bit tactless to enquire why *I* was elected. However, they were there for about five minutes con-gratulating me and asking me to do my best for the house before they left – quietly.

For a very long time I lay in the dark wondering if all this was some kind of vivid fantasy on my part. But I knew it wasn't. I was now in Debate. Here are the reasons why I was so astounded about the matter: to start with, I wasn't even a Specialist – not until the following term. And the rule, as I had known it, was that nobody could become a member of Debate until he was a Specialist. Never, in my knowledge, had this happened. Furthermore, election into Debate went just as much by seniority at work as a boy's respon-sibility. There were exactly eleven boys in the house who were senior to me, none of whom were in Debate, and five of them were

Specialists a term ahead of me. For these reasons my election was a thing I had not expected to happen for terms to come.

As I lay in bed and reflected on the whole matter, thoughts as to why I was elected hopped about in my head like fleas. There was something very unconvincing about the whole thing, I knew. I couldn't and refused to believe that any member of the Library or Debate could have even dreamt of the idea of electing me, because I was very unpopular and none of them really took to me. Before they got into Debate, I used to get into racial clashes now and again with many of them. Though they didn't now use their superior position to victimize me in any way, they rarely spoke to me and I knew that they still held their dislike. It seemed pathetic that they could have been prepared to waive aside the requirement for one to get into Debate and let me in, especially as it also meant a big queue barge. It seemed too unrealistic and illogical, particularly when I remembered that most of them had shown distaste when I was moved up to the senior table a few terms back.

Then a blazing light struck me – the whole thing must have been my housemaster's idea. I started to suspect strongly that there must have been a behind-the-scene chit-chat between him and the House Captain to allow me in. And why? . . . I could think of no other explanation except that it was because of my age and colour. Being nearly seventeen, I was the sixth oldest boy in my house. This to him, I fancied, made me old and responsible enough to be in Debate, on top of which I should be given the guest treatment because of my nationality, overlooking my low and academic position in the house. I felt very warmly towards my housemaster for his kind-heartedness.

It is unnecessary for me to describe the heat of the jealousy and fury that burnt boys senior to me in the morning when they found out about my election, especially among the Specialists. In the whole house, in fact, it was the centre of much talk and astonishment throughout the morning – during breakfast, along the landings, in the house library during Chambers, and no doubt in rooms. I didn't hear any blatant racial abuse uttered this time; but there were, from the jealous boys, obscene and bitter voices of disapproval and incredulity as to why I was elected. What damned absurdity was this? There were several hateful looks which I felt were full of racialism. The boys were now fed up! Obviously it seemed to them that this was just another allowance made simply because I was flaming well black! Here again, I felt they had every right to be bitter and angry, for which reason I wasn't hurt or put off by their hostile reaction; but it did make me feel rather uneasy, for I could sense that the dislike some held for me was now turning to hate. I should have perhaps said that two other boys were elected with me. But due to the great scandal that my election caused, very little notice was given to them.

Many boys outside my house heard about my election, and for a few days I was approached and asked about it all over the place, especially in division rooms. I used to be specifically asked, amid all the astonishment, why *I* had been elected, since I wasn't even a Specialist yet. I used to feel embarrassed and self-conscious, since I myself didn't for certain know why. It was worse still when, as happened on two different occasions, nearly the whole division room's attention was drawn, and boys crowded round my desk firing me with questions and making ape noises. With concealed discomfort, I expressed my suspicion that I must have been elected because of my age. This was always my reply at other places that I was asked. I would have felt too embarrassed to even dream of admitting my suspicion that my colour played a bigger part than my age. I felt, actually, that the boys were most likely thinking that. 'My God! You lucky beggar!' was the usual reply most of them could offer, punching the words. I could not fail to detect their envy about it, and justifiably enough, I felt; for, though they weren't in my house, most of them were senior to me, and I had reached a position of authority long before they hoped to in their houses. The fact that only very few of them congratulated me seemed to make their envy of the matter more obvious. They weren't angry, but I knew that if they were members of my house, they too would have been fuming.

Even boys I normally got on with were emotionally affected by my election. I recall that sometime during the afternoon on the day after it, I visited the room of one of them, where four boys were present. There was no hostility, but on the other hand, there were no cheerful faces. They all looked dull and I could read envy all over their faces. They returned my greeting very flatly. I plucked up enough courage to say in an understanding way that they were all, I supposed, angry about my election. There were a few hesitant 'well . . . ', followed by glances at each other, which to me all seemed a very tactful way of replying 'you can say that again!' Old Charles Coaker, my former mess mate joined in with a somewhat lazy voice and said,

'Well not all that much, so long as you don't become officious and go round fining us for everything we do wrong. Since we are really senior to you, it would be pretty mean of you.'

Everybody heartily agreed with him, and I assured them that I was well aware of that, and it would not be the case. That was okay with them, and soon the subject was changed: but not before somebody whom I can't quite recall also pointed out that it would be wrong for me to take action against them for two offences which, before my election, I had known were going on, and had occasionally committed myself.

Those offences were smoking and drinking, which had become quite usual among boys in the school, including members of the Library and Debate. When they smoked they did so in their own rooms or those of friends, sitting or kneeling around the fireplace and blowing the smoke up the chimney. They held empty match-boxes in which to put the ashes; and at the sound of approaching footsteps they would hurriedly put the cigarette ends into the box and the box into a pocket, then act casually. Quite a number of boys, a few of whom were in my house, were caught smoking and drinking during my time at the school, and the usual penalty was a beating by the Headmaster. Only a very few were dismissed.

Be that as it may, everybody in Plisnier's room had my assurance that I would overlook these offences, and they weren't to worry. I granted that their requests were fair and valid, but politely insisted that as a member of Debate, I would have to maintain a certain amount of responsibility and not allow them to continually misbehave and break all other rules. They were obliged to concede to that point.

I was determined to get to the bottom of the reason for my

election. It was all too baffling for words! I think it was in the afternoon two days after it took place that I visited the room of freckled Bobby Bell, a bright and pleasant member of the Library, popular with the lower boys for his leniency. On my entry he was lying on his bed listening to pop music blaring from his record player. He received me cheerfully and bade me turn down the record player and sit down. I did so and wasted no time in coming out directly with what was on my mind. With a tone of surprised interest I asked him candidly why I was elected into Debate. He answered that it was because it was felt I would make a jolly responsible member. Jokingly I told him to stop being absurd. He assured me that really was the case. What? I replied, and I'm not even a Specialist? And with so many boys senior to me? He replied that I was older than everybody else, and I looked the responsible sort. Quite amazed, I thanked him on behalf of the other members of the two authorities for electing me, and we were soon chatting about other topics. I didn't know what else to say on the matter. There was really nothing more I could say. I found his reasons too difficult to believe when I remembered that most of the Library and Debate had shown distaste at my moving up to the senior table because of my age. I didn't think it would be exactly in good taste to bring all that up to Bell.

I remained convinced that Bell was being patronizing and wasn't telling me the truth. I felt it was none other than my house-master's idea that I should be elected. My suspicions proved correct when, before long, a rumour started to circulate that I had been elected to cheer me up because I had not heard from my parents in Biafra for months and was worried that they might have been killed. When boys inside and outside my house mentioned this to me I always denied it. But, like an equation so simple that it was awesome, everything became clear. That rumour was, I realized, nothing less than the truth. That was why I was elected into Debate! I was now left in no doubt whatsoever that it was entirely my housemaster's idea.

After his first sitting in the International Court, my father had gone back to Biafra just before the war started at the end of May 1967. The Court was in recess for about a year, and for nearly all that time my father was in the breakaway state as the war raged. During that Summer term of 1967, he had written several times informing me of his safety. There was a land, sea and air blockade on Biafra, but there were still secret routes of entry and exit, and letters were put in care of people coming out to be posted abroad. That was how I got my mail. Naturally all the time that he was back there, I was living in a sea of fear and worry for his safety. This intensified when no more letters seemed to come from him the following term. Throughout that term nothing was heard of him; I was dreadfully afraid that he might have been killed. Gravely I used to express my fears to my housemaster when he came into my room. He appeared very sympathetic and kept trying to reassure me that most likely the post was being affected by the war growing more furious. As it happened, however, my father was totally unharmed and sometime around February 1968, he managed to get out of Biafra with my stepmother and two-year-old brother and returned to Holland. For various reasons he had been unable to write.

My housemaster was the *only* person to whom I expressed my fears about my father, and no boy. I vaguely recall telling a few boys that he was in Biafra and I was worried about him, but I *never* expressed my fear that he might have been killed. So I felt that it must have been that my housemaster's sympathy towards me grew to the extent that he was concerned about my happiness, and decided to cheer me up by giving me one hell of a surprise. So he instructed the House Captain to put me in Debate. Obviously he must have told him why he wanted me elected, and subsequently the rumour circulated.

I began to realize that the reason why the electors were so jovial and pleasant on the night they elected me was probably because the House Captain instructed them to be. Tom Peyton was his name, a tall, fairly harsh boy whom I knew had never liked me because of my aggressive manner. I have always been convinced that left to themselves, he and the rest among the two authorities wouldn't have dreamed of electing me. I suspected that they all thought it preposterous when they heard of my housemaster's instructions! But they had to yield hopelessly to the reality facing them: I was to be in Debate and there was absolutely nothing they could do about it but to accept it. I further suspected that Peyton instructed them to conduct the election properly and traditionally despite the absurdity of the situation, which meant that they were to be as cheerful as usual and not to show me in any way that this was one great fiddle to which they were, doubtless, very strongly opposed. So all the joviality and congratulations, I suspected, were insincere and just put on so as to conform to tradition.

One more suspicion I have always retained about the affair is that Peyton could have been instructed by my housemaster that I shouldn't be told the real reason of my election should I ask. And obviously Peyton informed the others of this. That seemed to explain why Bobby Bell didn't tell me the truth when I went and asked him.

I never met with any abuse or noticeable hostility from the other members of Debate or Library after my election. I didn't give thought as to the reasons, but in retrospect I feel that it was partly because they knew I was in Debate for good, so it would be pointless crying over spilt milk: and partly because it would be disgraceful to find members of Debate or Library in warfare against themselves, especially if it should be in full view of non-members, for they were supposed to be the house authorities and disciplinarians.

All the same, I had become aware of the way that most of them were boycotting me. I could go to hell as far as they were concerned! Their attitude was as if to say: 'Do what you want, but just keep away from me.' So without any hard feelings, I used to do that. Except for dull words of greeting sometimes when we passed each other, we didn't exchange dialogue very much unless it was necessary. I knew again that their distaste to my election was just as much because of my violent character as its unfairness to many boys, and had I been popular, they most likely wouldn't have minded so much, if at all. There were, however, a few members of the two authorities who were normally cheerful and always seemed ready to chat with me.

All went well my first term in Debate and I managed to help maintain order in the house without having to fine too many boys.

However, there were some common offences for which a fine was mandatory, such as being more than three minutes late for breakfast or leaving books on the slab before going to bed.

One thing I made sure I did was to fag boys. I was thrilled at the thought that I now had the power to do so, and on several occasions I sent fags down to buy me refreshments from the tuck shops or deliver messages to other houses. I never objected to boys in my block smoking or drinking, and indeed was often present, with other members of Debate, when they did so. This was a very risky business, for if a member of the Library entered suddenly and saw us condoning such offences, we would certainly smell hot trouble – most likely an indefinite suspension from Debate.

I remember that after my election into Debate, I used to consider thankfully how fortunate I was to have been put in my particular house. It occurred to me that not many housemasters would have treated me with so much more kindness and concern than the other boys. They probably would have held the view that I would fit in and get on better by being treated on the same level as everybody else, my colour being disregarded. Judging by the angry reactions of boys in my house as a result of the two special allowances made for me, I realized this was very much true. I was still happy, however, to have the embarrassment eased off about being the most junior in my house among the boys in my block. And I was grateful for the allowances more than I was enraged by the implications behind them.

My housemaster admired me a good deal for my games and used to encourage me when he visited my room during evenings.

Though he never in any way hinted it, I have always betted that
set in his mind was the old myth about black sporting prowess.
He did several good deeds for me that boys did not know about,
and I imagine that he would not have done them for others. On
several occasions of a holiday, for example, during the former half
of my time at the school, he had come into my room on the evening before and amiably persisted that I should go away from Eton
and enjoy myself: go on an outing for the whole day to London
or somewhere – because I was hardly ever visited or taken out by
anybody – so as to combat the tedium of being stuck in the school
all the time without a break. I used to reply reassuringly that I was
perfectly content to while the time away at the school, and didn't
care much to go anywhere. Usually I had my way, but occasionally I gave in to his persistence and said I would like to visit
London Airport. But that was not all: he always gave me permission to collect £2 from the dame to spend for the day. That would
go on my bill.

What a boy did on a holiday, I fancied, was none of his housemaster's concern. Whether or not he was a lonely soul, or never
taken out by anybody, a boy knew, of course, that a holiday was
an occasion when he could leave Eton and enjoy himself, and was
entirely master of his day. It would not be or should not be the
housemaster's business to suggest what he should do; after all, he
was surely old enough to look after himself and know what he
wanted without being mothered around. These points convinced
me again that my colour was the reason for my housemaster's
concern. What was more, if a boy was going away for the day, he
had to spend from his own pocket. He was *not* allowed to collect

money from the dame unless permission for him to do so had been given in advance by his parents. He could (and sometimes did) get packed lunch from the dame, but no money would be given to him. It was obvious that my case was different.

Another example of my housemaster's special treatment that I remember well happened in the summer of 1967. One way or another he had come to find out that I had never bothered to go to Lord's to watch the annual cricket match between Eton and Harrow. He came into my room the night before the match and mildly persuaded me to go. Being such a keen and good cricketer, he said, I should go and watch such a famous and interesting event instead of lounging around in the school all day doing nothing. I knew this was just another case of his concern for my happiness and finding something to do. I agreed to go, and he invited me to travel there and back with him in his car, since it was too late to get a seat in any of the school coaches. And on arriving at Lord's he paid for my entry and gave me two pounds for the day. Normally, boys who went to Lord's had to pay for all expenses out of their own money. I never knew if that money was to go on my bill or not since he never said anything about it. But somehow, I have been inclined to believe that it wasn't: he paid for me at his own expense. He didn't even bother to ask if I had any money of my own, which in fact I did have. The same applied to the occasions of holidays when he gave me permission to collect money from the dame to go away and enjoy myself.

Perhaps my housemaster need never have worried about my taking a break from Eton during the term, since the vacations were more than break enough. I had, until I left my guardian, mostly been going to stay at the vicarage and had spent most of the time fishing with my brother. I spent the next year holidaying with friends and relations in London until my father rented a house in The Hague at the end of 1967 and from then onwards Holland was always my destination. It was good to be living in a home with your family again after such a long time. Apart from my two-year-old brother, my other three brothers used to be there too. My elder brother had qualified as a doctor not long before the Nigerian civil war and was practising at Guy's Hospital in London; the one after me was at Millfield, the public school in Somerset, and the other was at a prep school in Hampshire – having come to England late in 1966. My sister was, fortunately enough, safe and sound in Biafra with relatives. We had found difficulty getting her out, but after I left Eton we eventually succeeded.

I did nothing especially interesting in The Hague: I occasionally fished the canals with some success and rambled along the busy streets. The occasional weekend family drives round Holland were pretty enjoyable. I didn't especially care to make many Dutch friends, but made one or two. I found the jolly Dutch, on the whole, more reserved and easy-going than English people, and my family was extremely impressed by the remarkable tidiness and cleanliness with which they kept their country.

I had had a chance to visit other European countries during parts of holidays. In the Easter of 1966, I went with the school's cast of *Caesar and Cleopatra* to Germany. We went for two weeks during the holidays to stage a performance in West Berlin, at a mixed school called Schiller Schule. It was a delightful stay, and we made numerous pleasant excursions round West and East

Berlin. We also attended several concerts and parties. A few members of the cast stayed with the masters and make-up team in a hotel, but most of us stayed with German families. Mine was Family Sprott, a middle-aged couple with a very shapely and pretty fifteen-year-old daughter, named Vera. A most charming and entertaining family, the father was a baker, the mother a housewife and Vera a student of Schiller Schule. We could communicate perfectly well, though they couldn't speak English very well. Their comfortable flat was on top of their fair-sized shop, and their bakery within. And every night Vera, a shy, smiling girl with dark shoulder-length hair, placed a plate containing half a dozen delicious cakes by my bedside. I will never forget the kindness of that family.

Our visit had attracted the German press. A few days after our arrival, a photographer came and snapped away during a rehearsal one evening. On two different occasions illustrated articles appeared in an evening paper; and, by chance, one of them was of me kneeling before Cleopatra as a Nubian sentinel. It was a pleasant surprise.

In the course of my time at Eton I went to Italy and Denmark during the summer holidays, visiting Rome and Copenhagen. I spent only a few weeks at each, but they were much enjoyed ones – spent mostly sight-seeing. I stayed with Biafran friends of my family. I visited Copenhagen alone, and Rome with my younger brother.

I only visited my own country once during my time at Eton, and that was early on in summer 1965. It was the first time I had been back for two years, since my father had visited England the year in between. I went with my younger brother, for eight weeks. It was great to be back home once again – back in the wonderful sun among friends and loved ones. I suppose that I had become quite Anglicized after six years in England. But not enough to lose my racial identity, by any means. I could still speak my own language fluently; I was still very familiar with the customs, habits and ways of life etc. of my own people, and so I found no difficulty in reintegrating. I need not describe my feeling of sorrow when the time to leave for England eventually came – to leave the warmth and friendship of my motherland and return to the cruel biting frosts of a freezing winter, and return to Eton, a place where I had fitted in badly and become disliked. It was an awesome feeling as well.

That was the last time I went back home. After the first military *coup d'état* in Nigeria at Christmas 1965, another followed in the summer of 1966, after which years of bitter strife and dreadful bloodshed were to follow. It would have been suicidal to ever go back there.

The one thing I never did during the holidays was work. Work was for school only, and holidays were for complete relaxation. That was how I saw it. Holidays too were times when one should forget all about school, I thought. So I used to try to completely forget about Eton and everything to do with it; which was a bit surprising, for, being a snob and proud to be a member of the world's most famous school, I would have always felt keen to talk a lot and show off about it, I thought. However, that was not the case during the holidays.

So much for my housemaster's concern for my happiness because I was hardly taken out, and no doubt inspired because I hardly saw my parents. I might mention that my father had come on two occasions to see me at Eton and take me out: once just before he went to Biafra and again after he had come out safe and sound. He came on both occasions with my elder brother. The first time they came was on a non-half-day, and my housemaster kindly allowed me to miss the final division and go out to tea with them. It was a fine summer afternoon, and I remember that, as we returned from tea in Windsor in the chauffeur-driven Humber hired from London, the last division finished and the boys flocked the streets on their way to tea. My father seemed particularly interested in and impressed by certain boys – the 'collegers', colloquially known as 'tugs'. They always attended divisions with gowns over their uniforms, which made them look so highly important and learned. Those two words are most certainly the right ones to describe them. They were among the seventy boys who had been awarded scholarships and lived in the original College building. Their fees were largely remitted, and they took the title K S – King's Scholar – after their names. Their house, College, as it was referred to by boys, was not counted among the school's twenty-five houses.

My father was impressed with the scholars because they were 'brains'. Like the average African father, he was obsessed with boys doing well at school, greatly admiring the brainy ones. I leave it to one to imagine his distaste at my continued bad progress at Eton. But, all the same, I knew that he was proud to be the father of a black Etonian. When we were in the Humber looking out at the boys, off to their houses, he kept saying that we were certainly kept very healthy and fit. I knew that it was because of his admiration for the school that he said that really. Most likely we weren't any more healthy than any other school – just more privileged, and more coolly and sophisticatedly dressed. And, above all, more famous.

Chapter Nine
Violence

From what I have written, it would be correct to assume that colour prejudice was the most outstanding feature of my experiences at Eton. The general impression no doubt gathered is that I was always the innocent victim of it. To be more explicit, that I was always abused first before hitting out, and never provoked boys myself. This was mostly the case, but not always. There were occasions when I could not resist the temptation to provoke and tease boys just for the thrills of it and in so doing was greeted, deservedly enough, with insults. For example, when I used to hold boys in bear-hugs, etc., with the knowledge that they deplored it. There was, however, one particular event of some significance that I recollect.

One morning during my third term, I clashed with red-faced Tim, a fair, very nervous and shy fellow who would burst into sudden hysterical temper when teased too much. This happened on a few of the occasions that boys made fun of him in division rooms, and anybody who got too close to him would be clouted pretty hard. There were two reasons why boys made fun of him: firstly, because of the way he faltered self-consciously as he read to the division whenever a master asked him to, and because of his good friendship with another boy which, by and by, became suspected as a sexual one. I came to rather enjoy seeing him angry, and started feeling the urge to provoke him myself one day. On the occasion we clashed, he had managed to quietly but with unconcealed pain and misery, sit through the taunts from a group of boys. After division, as everybody dashed off for Chambers, I remained behind to ask the master something about the work he had set us. Tim too stayed behind, still taking down notes from the board, deliberately, I suspected, for fear that boys would wait for him outside to finish off their taunts. However, the master soon departed, leaving me alone with him. A few seconds later he picked up his books, greeted me, and was on his way out. I called him to hold on as he reached the door, and approached with my books. Then I brought up the rumour about his alleged sexual friendship with a boy. Blushing hotly, he assured me it wasn't true. Just for the joy of rousing his anger, I persisted that it was true and pointed out that he was blushing. Suddenly a hateful look came to his slightly rocky-chinned face. He briefly eyed me in silence, then quietly, in a throaty and somewhat tearful voice, warned: 'Look, Onyeama, you stop saying that.' And the next second I felt such an almighty punch to my chin, that I was jolted against the wall. Before I knew what exactly struck me, he was off down the big wooden passage at great speed. I stood there staunching the trickle of blood from my lips with a handkerchief – in paralysed disbelief. The element of speed and surprise had indeed been brought to play. I never expected this; and being black and much bigger than he was, I never dreamt that he would dare touch me, let alone half dislocate my jaw. It took me a long time to overcome the pain of the surprise. I did feel, however, that I had deserved that blow since I had provoked him, and I never sought to return it. As a matter of fact, in another division room that day he came and apologized to me – more than anything else, I felt, out of fear and worry of what I might do to him. The apologies were mutual, and I confessed that I had been at fault. From that day onwards, I left him alone. He himself had never, as far as I can recall, abused me in any way.

The fact that he himself was teased now and again, and hated it, shows that I wasn't the only boy to be continually picked on at Eton. Of course, there were a number of boys who were often teased and ragged for various reasons, and some deplored it. But all the same, I would very much doubt whether anybody else attracted quite the degree of abuse, hostility and personal opprobrium as seemed to be my lot.

I have always remembered that incident with Tim in particular, because no other boy that I had conflicted with ever dared to hit me half as hard as he did; and the few that occasionally struck me when I struck them, always did so on my arm. The incident shows, however, that I wasn't the only boy capable of hitting people hard when tormented.

When they used to jeer in division rooms, my tormentors sometimes betted that I would never dare to hit somebody of my own size and strength who racially abused me. They used to bitterly express their wish that somebody bigger and stronger than I was would one day slog the daylights out of me. I always replied that I would hit anybody at all despite his strength, though I knew that wasn't quite true.

There were a good number of boys at the school who were my size and a good number who were bigger. But nearly all those who abused me were smaller. Only a few were bigger than I was – mostly those who had caught up and overtaken me in size as the terms passed; but all the same I sometimes hit them as well. And funnily enough, it was they of all people who never dared hit me back, because, I felt, of fear that I might use the excuse that they were bigger than me to savagely thump them. Speaking truthfully, I was never racially abused by anybody whom I didn't think I could beat up, nor would be afraid to hit. In my junior terms, I knew of course that there were boys who could beat me up in a fight, and until I left it wouldn't have surprised me if that was still the case: there were always some powerful-looking characters whom I wasn't sure if I would defeat or not. But I had come to believe with confidence that few boys in the school would be keen to take me on because of my size and colour, and because of my reputation of being the school's heavyweight boxing champion. I knew, however, that I would think twice before making an aggressive move towards an abuser whom I wasn't sure about. I would most certainly have abused him back, then, engaging in verbal conflict with him, guess from his reactions whether he was at all afraid of me or would strike me back with full confidence. If the former, I would have threatened him with violence if he abused me again; if the latter, I would continue arguing with him. But I was positive of one thing: if, for some reason, my temper got out of control, I would certainly have reacted as Tim did to me. No matter how big you may be, how strong or whatever colour, one would care for absolutely nothing when driven to uncontrollable temper – except the full satisfaction of expressing one's blind madness by powerfully belting, and damn whatever fate one may suffer as a result. Unlike Tim, I wouldn't have run away, but made a hell of a fight out of it.

However, my tormentors' candid wish that I would one day be beaten up by somebody stronger than me never came true. I well remember, too, something similar they used to say, 'Why don't you fucking well pick on someone your own size and colour?' And, 'I'd love to see the day another big black wog would thump the bloody hell out of you!' I can remember with sharp clarity the four boys who, on different occasions, shouted remarks like these at me in division rooms. They never stated why it should be a black person to beat me up and not an Etonian. They didn't need to, for I knew perfectly well; and I felt that they expected me to know: white boys would be no match for me. Though, I'm sure, they didn't mean it to be, I found that rather flattering.

The word 'wog' which I have just mentioned in passing was one racial name which I always seemed to fear at Eton. Together with 'nig-nog', it was the term of abuse which, as I said earlier, I did not, to start with, understand the meaning of. I had thought it referred to my plump figure, and I took it to mean something like 'fat pig'. When, by and by, I came to find out that it was a racial name, I deplored it yet more. It bothered and infuriated me more than any other form of their racial abuse. There was something so distasteful about the word, something devilish. Whether it was the way it was pronounced or whatever, I have never been exactly sure why I hated the word. In retrospect I feel it could be for two possible reasons: first, because it conjured up thoughts of a longer, more unpleasant word – 'golliwog' – an evil-looking, black toy with fuzzy hair, and secondly, because wog was directed at me so often. In fact, it was the most usual taunt I received; and every time it was used against me, an electric shock surged through my body, tormenting my senses.

The word, together with all the other racial abuse I was experiencing, helped in driving me beyond breaking point. My tormentors were easily getting the better of me on the abuse-and-violence dispute, and their persistent abuse had become too much for my mind to take. I became fed up, bitter and frustrated, and as a result started having fits of violence. The fits began during the summer of my third year, and to start with were pretty frequent. Sometimes they took place in the afternoon, other times in the evening, and I can remember the details as clearly as I read the words I write. I would be slumped in my armchair, totally unaware of the world outside, and torturing my mind by intently casting it back on all the racial hostility that I had been experiencing in division rooms. Vividly the painful pictures of my tormentors and their jeers slowly repeated themselves on my mind again and again. I pictured them laughing derisively at my useless retaliation, uttering racial abuse. I pictured myself standing there being tormented, frustrated and full of hate, yet helpless and unable to use violence over them due to the overwhelming odds. That dreaded word 'wog' was being persistently blasted from their lips. And as I sat there I was filled with anguish, and a dire hate for all white people. Suddenly I could see nothing good in them at all. Only half-conscious of them, tears of bitterness and pain welled up in my eyes. My mind became a mass of confusion. Heavy anger filled me; and at the apex of my anger, my tormentors stood there, jeering and laughing unmercifully. Suddenly I could stand it no longer. 'Wog' and all their other names scraped along my nerves until I longed to scream hysterically and break the tension coiled like a spring within me. My eyes screaming murder, my blood at boiling point, I suddenly leapt to my feet like a madman. With black rage I started mercilessly slogging thin air, imagining I had charged at my tormentors and was beating the hell out of a particular one. The whole thing seemed as if it was really happening, though I knew, of course, that it was not: I was beating up somebody who was not there, but was grimly delighted to imagine that he was there. The room was quaking as, in my uncontrollable wildness and berserk actions, I kicked and struck out with all my might at my invisible tormentor. And at the same time, with the rage that my throat begged to roar, I hissed out obscene, racial abuse and gasps, the latter in an effort to stack more power in my swinging fists and legs. In the seething welter of my emotions, I was, however, able to stifle the noise of my voice so as not to attract outside attention. Then with a last gasp of anguish, I delivered the demon punch and it all ended. Next I stood there, sweating, panting, my chest heaving, looking down at the disarranged carpet, as if looking down with grim satisfaction at a motionless body lying in a great pool of blood – dead or unconscious. For about ten seconds I would stand there, and then with a sinking heart and bitter regret, come to acknowledge the reality that this was all child's play. I had only beaten up my tormentor in my mind, and whatever happened, I bitterly knew, he and his partners would always continue their taunts. I knew I wouldn't dare attack any of them as madly as I had done mentally, for fear of what harm I might do. On realizing all this, I would with a hopeless sigh go and collapse in my armchair, and still breathing almost hysterically, try and cool down my temper.

These fits used to last for a good thirty seconds. And as the days passed, and I kept having the hallucinations of my jeering persecutors, I became more and more violent-minded, and my bitterness against them intensified. As a result, my fits became a more dangerous and bloodthirsty affair, so that anybody who might have entered the room at those calamitous moments, may well have ended up a very dead and mutilated heap. For, instead of pounding thin air with my fists and feet, I started using my cricket bat. Wild-eyed and like the demon of wrath and vengeance, I held the bat by the handle and swung it all over the room – subconsciously careful not to smash any breakables at the same time. On this occasion I was swinging at *all* my tormentors, and as they scattered in dread, I managed to clobber one of them to the ground. As he lay there screaming and writhing in nerve-searing agony, I stood over him and with malicious delight mingled with extreme hate, I unmercifully beat down upon his body and skull until every ounce of his life was crushed out of him. Due to the great noise it would have made, I never allowed my bat to actually strike the ground as I bore down on the invisible blood-spattered tormentor. Then after all that, back to my armchair to almost cry my temper away, terribly frustrated as well.

And when my chance actually did come in division rooms to

deal with my tormentors as I did in my imagination, I saw the great difference between fantasy and reality.

And so helplessly I continued with my hallucinations and fits, until eventually the former landed me in the most humiliating situations. They started tormenting me at other places apart from my room. On my bath nights, I found myself unable to get into my bath because of them. Shame to take off my clothes seemed to overwhelm me; for, as well as jeering at me, my tormentors were mockingly laughing and pointing at the fact that I was about to undress – as if I was going to perform a shameful and degrading act by revealing my naked body. Unmercifully their faces hammered my mind; and I restlessly stood in the small bathroom in my pyjamas and dressing-gown, thrown into frantic but subdued soliloquy, swearing and telling myself reassuringly that nobody was watching me, striving desperately to dispel the faces. All this used to go on for ten minutes until I summoned up enough courage to undress and get into my bath. On other occasions I only succeeded in dispelling my hallucinations because I suddenly became aware that time was passing, glanced at my watch and realized with horror that I only had five minutes to get in and out of the bath and wash it out (we were allowed fifteen minutes in the bath). And a few times I never had my bath at all. I just stood there in my agitated state until the next boy after me banged on the door to hurry me up. I had been completely unaware of the time.

The same things used to happen in the lavatory and when I had to undress in my room for games, for bed at night and for breakfast in the morning. In fact, whenever I seemed to be alone in quietude I was always wrestling with my hallucinations. I used to have difficulty in sitting down to concentrate on set work to be learnt or written, and it usually took me a long time to complete it. I kept getting up from my chair and walking up and down my room mouthing an agitated soliloquy. Then suddenly I realized that I had better complete my work or I'd be in serious trouble with the master, and I sat down and was able to concentrate without breaking off. And the reason I kept getting up was because it suddenly seemed as if my room was some kind of a hall, sometimes a division room, where all my enemies in the school were standing; they were all jeering 'filthy wog' at me because I had the bad manners to be sitting instead of standing. As a result of these hallucinations, I did a few times jump up suddenly from my chair and madly punch thin air instead of soliloquizing.

The same visions haunted me as I lay in my bed after lights-out: something about my lying down seemed immoral and so my tormentors jeered and abused me, I was too lazy to get out of bed and start punching thin air: instead I just tossed and turned, cursing with irritation and bitterness, and as a result it used to take me hours to eventually get off to sleep.

My hallucinations were occurring, honestly, every single day. The fits were nothing like as frequent, but as I said, were quite frequent to begin with. It was the former which bothered me most, since they were so persistent and provoked the fits. And sometime in the latter part of the term they had begun, I felt that something had to be done to put an end to them. I used to give the matter serious thought, and in the back of my mind lurked the horrible feeling that I was going mad. I decided to go and tell the dame, and see what she could suggest. But I had first racked my brains as to how and what exactly I would tell her. I just felt too embarrassed at the thought of mentioning my fits, so that was scrubbed! And I certainly had no intention of saying that it was all the racial abuse in the school that caused everything, for I feared that she would inevitably notify my housemaster, and a lot of trouble and enquiries would begin. I finally decided to tell her about the hallucinations only and the ways they troubled me. That was what I did. After supper one night I went to the small medicine-room and joined the eight or so noisy boys waiting inside and outside. When it was my turn, it was with the utmost sheepishness that I confronted the dame.

'Ma'am, it may sound odd, but I'm suffering from persecution complex.'

Her face crumpled into a puzzled frown.

'Persecution complex?' she asked in her Scottish accent.

'W—Well, yes, Ma'am,' I smiled with embarrassment.

'Who's persecuting you?'

She got me there. I stuttered a bit as I searched for a reply. All the boys present started to listen with interest.

'W—W—Well, Ma'am, nobody exactly, Ma'am,' I lied.

'My dear boy,' she normally addressed us thus, 'what on earth do you mean?'

Giggles resounded from the other boys at her baffled question. My heart beat like African tom-toms, and boiling with humiliation I answered:

'Well, I don't know what you can call it, Ma'am; but every time I go to undress I can't, Ma'am, because I keep seeing faces watching me and laughing.'

Loud, almost derisive laughter resounded this time, and the dame had to call sharply for silence. She then faced me again. Her puzzled expression intensified, and she looked at me as if a few stains of madness must have soiled my brain. She was a slim and trim woman of average height, pleasant and talkative. Though popular with boys on the whole, it was felt she was too fussy; always fussing at such things as untidy rooms, noise and whether boys refused any course at lunch, though we weren't compelled to eat everything.

'Faces watching you?' she asked.

'Yes, Ma'am. It sounds odd, Ma'am, but that's the situation. I just can't undress when I want to have my bath or get into bed because I keep on picturing these faces watching me. And I also find it impossible to get to sleep, Ma'am.'

The laughter that now shook everybody's body was muffled by their hands.

'Oh!' returned the dame, really taken aback, and seemingly lost as to what to say. 'Oh,' she repeated and then paused slightly. Then, 'Do you know who these people are watching you?'

'W–W–Well, Ma'am, just different boys in the school.'

'How peculiar.' Her voice sank lower. 'I just don't know what to say. Can't you get them off your mind?'

'No, Ma'am,' I replied somewhat assuringly. 'I don't know why,' I lied, 'but I just keep picturing their faces.'

Again she paused, and then shook her head hopelessly.

'My dear boy, all I can say is stop thinking about them. There's nothing *I* can do.' Her face brightened as she spoke. 'I can't drive them away for you.' She then laughed. Everybody did likewise, and I forced another smile of embarrassment. 'If nobody's actually watching you, I don't see what you've got to worry about. You've just got to try not to think about them.'

Shrugging my shoulders I replied submissively, 'I'll try, Ma'am.' I then thanked her and left.

And truly I was ever so thankful to leave, and felt bitter regret at having gone in there. I had felt such a ridiculous fool telling her all that, so small and childish. I cursed myself for not having had the intelligence to foresee that my complaint was going to sound ridiculously funny to the boys and inevitably expose me to great embarrassment. I knew I should have waited till the dame made her visits to rooms at bedtime and told her alone. I have never completely lived down the embarrassment of that confrontation, and I can hardly bring myself to think about it. More embarrassing still was that the matter circulated in the house, and for the next few days I was being approached by rather amused boys and asked: 'What's all this I hear that you can't undress and have your bath because you keep seeing faces staring at you?' Boys outside my house obviously heard about it, for in the streets, a few put similar questions to me. I irritably told them all to get lost and forget it, without giving an answer. I don't recall ever discussing the matter with any boy.

However, for the next week after my visit to the dame, she visited my room a few times during her rounds. She always asked me if I was still seeing these faces. And I always said yes, as indeed had been the case. Baffled, she never used to say anything much more than that she couldn't imagine what the matter could be, and that I would have to keep trying to dispel these thoughts. There must be a reason why I must keep thinking people were staring at me? I always lied that there was no reason whatsoever. I recall that she once asked me if it could be that I was doing something I shouldn't be doing. I gave a firm negative reply.

She informed my housemaster of my troubles. And round about ten o'clock one night, he came into my room as I was actually having my hallucinations. Without turning on the light he stood at the door, apologized in case he should have woken me up, and said that the dame had told him I kept having difficulty getting to sleep. If this continued, he said, I should come down to his study and have a chat with him. His voice was gentle and somewhat comforting, and after I agreed to his request, he left. His visit dispersed my hallucinations, and I lay in bed thinking over what he said. I knew that the dame must have told him everything, and I wasn't altogether happy about it, because I would never have wanted to tell him what was behind it all, for the sake of peace and quiet. Also, I felt, it would be a cowardly way of getting my abusers to stop their taunts. I suspected that he probably felt I was very frustrated about something, and perhaps by amicably talking to me and trying to find out my problem, the tension could be eased. Much as I felt grateful at his wish to help me, I had no intention whatsoever of ever going down to speak to him.

As I reflected on all this that night, I decided that from now on, I would start telling the dame that my hallucinations were diminishing and were no longer worrying me. Simply because if I kept saying the reverse, it could well lead to a lot of questioning by my housemaster in an attempt to find out what really was bothering me. I felt that he would most likely suspect that I would be too afraid or embarrassed to come out with the truth. It all seemed too close for comfort.

So for the next week, I was always bright-faced whenever the dame visited my room, and told her exactly what I had planned to say. Eventually I said, untruthfully, that my hallucinations had completely gone. So the matter was forgotten. But for me, it certainly wasn't and couldn't be forgotten. They had gone on every day, and to keep them going, there was racial abuse in division rooms and other parts of the school. The fits became occasional now: I had managed to get more control over myself. And as the terms went by, they became quite rare. The hallucinations, however, went on ceaselessly until I left the school. Even throughout the holidays I just couldn't stop thinking about all the hurtful racial abuse in the school. I don't recall ever having fits during the holidays.

However, the most important thing that I had always wanted since my hallucinations began started to occur two or three terms later: I started to become unaffected by them when undressing, working and trying to sleep. Even though the faces were always there, laughing and jeering, I couldn't care less. Without the least hesitation or embarrassment, I would just scornfully let them continue and quietly proceed with whatever it was I wanted to do. I had forcibly told myself to grow up! I knew full well that they were just fantasies – even though they were damned annoying and frustrating. However, as my last year slowly passed, I was able to overcome them, become less and less worried by them, and the tension greatly eased.

Chapter Ten
Witchcraft, Black Power and Other Happenings

During my last year, things started to happen and change at Eton, especially in my house. Until I had been elected to Debate, the Permissive Society, of which we read so much in the newspapers, had had very little effect on the way of life in the school. Things were still regulated by traditions and customs of many years' standing. But after the term of my election, and for the next three while I was at the school, the atmosphere did change completely in my house.

This started with a new House Captain whose name was Mark Blackett-Ord. He had always been a very popular member of the Library because of his leniency and good humour. When he became Captain, there was general ease and happiness, particularly among the lower boys, because he was strongly opposed to House Captains and Pops being allowed to beat boys. He felt that there were better methods of discipline than beatings, though he did accept that there had to be some means of controlling malefactors. That, of course, was what boys liked to hear, especially the mischievous ones. It meant that they could now do what they wanted and get away with it; whereas, before, there were strict and ruthless members of the Library who were only too happy to get them bending over a chair for offences like shirking boy-calls, frequent mobbing or rudeness. All these offences gradually worsened a great deal after Blackett-Ord became House Captain. Matters became pretty serious when, halfway through his first term in power, he abolished boy-calls altogether – with the consent of the housemaster, of course. What's more, he minimized the Debate's fagging privileges to the extent that it was hardly meaningful. We could now only fag boys on half-days, and had to obtain Blackett-Ord's permission any other time, and then only for very good reasons like, for instance, finding out from a boy in another house what was the work a master had set for a given date. The same changes applied for members of the Library, but they could still continue having personal fags for their rooms. When we were all summoned to the Library late one night and told of these changes by Blackett-Ord, our voices rose in a crescendo of indignation, protest, moans and grumbles, but to no avail. That privilege of delivering boy-calls which most of us had dearly looked forward to one day, was now, to our fury and disappointment, defunct. In fact, we had to admit that fagging was an obstacle to boys who were working, which was why Blackett-Ord had decided to minimize it. And the new rules weren't only to apply while he was Captain, but for good. That was the case with all rules made by House Captains.

Naturally, the fags were uncontrollably delighted when they saw the new rules on the noticeboards, and thundered vociferously around, chanting Blackett-Ord's praises, while members of Debate, myself included, bellowed at them to cut out the din or be fined.

He was a very talkative fellow, Mark Blackett-Ord, of medium size, with a mop of long, brown hair, and wore glasses. He spoke in an aristocratic manner, and walked somewhat wildly with a sway. Until he became House Captain, he and I hardly spoke and had nothing in common. He wasn't the quarrelsome or abusive type, but I knew he didn't like my character. After he became House Captain we started to get more amicable, but on a very superficial level; I could still sense that he didn't favour me. He left the same term as I did.

I myself had no particular views about discipline, but I strongly felt it was wrong that he should have let everyone know that he was opposed to discipline, particularly beatings. During social chats in rooms, several of us used to passionately discuss how grossly insolent and disrespectful to members of Debate the lower boys were becoming, and express our wish that Blackett-Ord would become stricter. Even though we usually got the better of them, with difficulty, this was the sort of problem that kept occurring: a member would come across a group of lower boys mobbing in a passage or in a room and shout at them to cut it out, otherwise they would be heavily fined! Sometimes they would ignore him with scorn and continue their racket, and the infuriated member, finding that he was merely wasting his breath, would be forced to go and pull them apart, cursing at them as he did so. Then there would be some sort of cheeky retort like, 'Okay then, go and fucking well fine us if you like! Who bloody well cares?' They would walk off, muttering and often refuse to come back when called, leaving the enraged member swearing bitterly to himself as he clattered off to find the fines book. And moreover, it was not only the lower boys who were the headaches; we had the same trouble with the older ones who were not in Debate.

It was during my last term that things really got out of hand. We had moved into another house that term. It was called Hodgson House and was situated on the High Street next to Alden and Blackwell, the stationers; a very old building with creaky floorboards and narrow staircases and passages, for which reason nobody liked it at all. Also, being on the High Street, we lived in predominant noise. Waynflete, our old house, was to undergo two terms of enlargement and reconstruction in many parts, after which my house would move back in again with its new master. His name was Oliver Bull, a big, thick-haired man of about my height, married with several children. Aged about forty, he taught Classics and was very musical: well known in the school for his jazz group consisting of boys, which now and again performed in School Hall. This plus his patient and cheerful character, earned him considerable respect and popularity. Boys found him too pleasant and inoffensive to want to offend him as they did other patient masters. Good-humoured, he was said to retain an open mind about many things. Most of the boys in my house were delighted when it became known a year before the Reverend Wild retired, that he was the one to take over. I had hardly known him myself, but in that one term I lived with him, I came to see the reason for his popularity. He was indeed very friendly and talkative, and I took to him quite a lot. He gave me no indication that he wanted to treat me any different from the others.

However, the goings-on in his house became quite a scandalous affair; for as the fear and respect for members of the Library and

Debate declined, so did the wish of these two authorities to assert themselves. They came to believe that boys should be allowed to express their views about anything, could misbehave, and be controlled with punishments which were not harsh. The view that it could all be done with kindness and good relationship was often expressed in Blackett-Ord's big, scantily decorated room. There, about nine or so boys would noisily congregate while the fags tidied the room, to chat, joke and drink coffee. The fags too would join in the amusement and conversation, expressing agreement and their own ideas, and speaking freely in obscene language. I used to be present in the happy atmosphere a few times, and was content to just sit down and listen without saying much, just uttering words of agreement now and again on a point. I had my own mixed feelings about the matter. I had been a lower boy myself once, and all the time hated and cowered under the sadistic members of the Library and Debate, so I felt that the lower boys did deserve some kindness and freedom for a change, and more mild control. On the other hand, though, I felt that in return we were entitled to a certain degree of respect, reasonable behaviour and less abuse from them. That by no means had been the case.

On being black, I had found no more difficulty controlling the junior boys than the other members of Debate, nor did I meet with any more abuse than they did. But being very colour conscious, I had always been worried that I was bound to meet with racial abuse in the new permissive life. That did happen, but fortunately only occasionally. While angrily trying to separate rowdy characters threatening them with fines, one of them would come out with blatant racial abuse, quite boldly and scornfully like, 'Oh damn you, you black wog!' My feelings were painfully pierced by this. Just as bad was the reaction of the other boys. Their smiles vanished abruptly and I was faced with very embarrassing stares, silent and somewhat apprehensive. It was as if they knew that something matchlessly offensive and serious had been said and wondered what might be my explosive reaction. But my reaction was nil. As the abuser walked off merrily, I just ignored him and angrily warned his friends that they would be heavily fined if I caught them mobbing again. In no way did I show that I had been affected by the slur of their friend. Much as it hurt me, I felt that being a prefect I couldn't possibly reveal its effect. With all the respect for us taken away by the introduction of permissiveness into the house, there was really nothing I could do about it. But the last thing I felt I should do was make them believe their friend had triumphed or made any impact. I just maintained the traditional stiff upper lip and gave them the impression that the abuse did not matter to me at all.

However, the result of the decline in the wish of the Library and Debate to assert themselves was that they could very often not care less how boys misbehaved. I myself started to do the same. I have to admit that this was partly because I always felt a bit afraid to give orders for fear that I might meet with some racial abuse. And the other reason was my knowledge that permissiveness, whether it was a good thing or a bad thing, had established itself firmly in the house with rather unfavourable consequences, and there was really nothing that could be done about it, except accept it and live with it. So unless there was really excessive noise, I rarely took much notice of mobbing and shouting; the same applied to other offences like disgraceful appearance, scribbling on the noticeboards and boys being present in rooms during the absence of the owners. Only a few members of the two authorities – the quiet, unsociable types who were strongly against Blackett-Ord's views – continued to bellow at and fine boys they caught misbehaving. And nearly always the boys answered back insolently, with the knowledge that nothing worse than a fine would happen to them.

What made them more positive of this, despite their knowledge that Blackett-Ord was against beating, was when he abolished beating in the house for good. This occurred around the middle of term several days after we had a debate in the Library late one night about corporal punishment. The idea had been on his mind for quite some time, but he wanted to first find out what all the members of the Library and Debate thought about it and how many agreed. It had been a highly interesting debate lasting an hour with many strong arguments. Out of the sixteen members of Debate and Library, however, about thirteen of us were against corporal punishment and supported his idea to abolish it. We were particularly against the idea of Pops and House Captains being allowed to beat, since they were also boys themselves, paying the fees and there to learn as well. It was felt they were too young to beat, and that only the masters, if anybody at all, should do it. I recall that I put in an opinion against beating, saying that it could have the wrong effect on boys and make them sadistic and full of hate.

When it was written up on the noticeboards, the abolition created considerable jubilance among the lower boys, who now knew categorically that no future House Captain could beat them. It also caused quite a stir outside the house. The national press got information of the matter, though it took them a long time to get it. At least a week later, a fairly lengthy piece appeared in the *Evening Standard* and the *Daily Telegraph*. They reported that corporal punishment by House Captains seemed to be diminishing at Eton. Apparently other houses had not used it for a very long time; but Hodgson House was the first to officially abolish it. My house was named, and my new housemaster made a statement saying that his senior boys were very keen on the idea. He personally did not mind and was prepared to give it a try and see how things went. I do recall that Blackett-Ord was mentioned as being the House Captain.

There was quite some gossip in many parts of the school following the newspaper publicity, my house being mostly the centre of it all. And inside my house itself, a good deal of excitement and speculation as to who informed the press. But it was never known.

So first it was boy-calls, then beating: two of the most detested aspects of Eton's traditions were now abolished. It was not more than two weeks after he abolished beating, however, that Blackett-Ord abolished yet another important tradition – fining.

Just for the information, the money from fines went on the Library's account for messing. They used to make quite a bit from fines and so were pretty well off for food. As for the Pops, the money went in their pockets. However, fining had never really been effective, and that was why Blackett-Ord decided to abolish it. He didn't have a debate about it this time, but occasionally discussed it with members of the two authorities in his room. No matter how often they were fined, wrongdoers continued their pranks; fining didn't really worry them, after all it was only money. So, with my housemaster's permission, Blackett-Ord substituted it with a points system, which actually was more disliked. This was more or less 'black marks' really. The points were marked down, together with the boy's name and offence, in a notebook kept in Blackett-Ord's room. A member of the Library or Debate could give as many points as he thought a boy's offence deserved. Those who scored four in a week were confined to their rooms and had to write an essay for Mosedale. If the points number got overwhelmingly high, they had to stay in longer or were given tedious tasks like sweeping the courtyard. The smallest boys were sent on early morning runs. Much as this was an unpopular system, it didn't have any noticeable effect on behaviour at all.

All the misbehaviour and indiscipline, however, was by no means among only the more junior boys of the house: long before beating was abolished, it had spread to and involved members of the Library and Debate themselves. They started engaging in all sorts of foolery, and not only among themselves but also with junior boys. This involved smoking and drinking, and the good relationship that was talked about in Blackett-Ord's room. The friendship between the older boys and the younger became so good that it almost boiled down to what my first housemaster disapproved of so strongly: big boys associating with little boys because of sexual attraction. The use of Christian names between the two groups became common, and they spoke and associated with each other as though they were in the same age or work group. One often came across a member of Debate or Library, usually the former, mobbing together in a passage with a younger non-member in full view of other boys, who often barracked them noisily. If it developed into a tussle, as was sometimes the case, with one of them bear-hugging the other a sea of amazed faces would fill the air together with cries of 'My God! Look at that! Bloody queer! Scandal!'

I have to admit that I was the same as the others. I had some part to play in the decline in behaviour of the two authorities. I befriended a few boys from two to four years younger than I was. And though I often released my temper and fined them, I allowed them to call me by my Christian name, speak to me as they wished, smoke in their rooms, visit my room, and mobbed with them.

This general decline in the standards of behaviour was not confined to my house. In one case, certainly, it was very much more scandalous and dramatic. There was one very popular housemaster whom I shall call Mr Nash, a slightly bald man, tall, well-built and of middle age. Smoking, getting drunk, and in drunken states molesting little boys in their rooms late in the night – for offences like these, nearly all the members of his Library were dismissed from the school, and a few of the Debate were beaten by the Headmaster. Mr Nash himself was told by the Headmaster that it would be in the best interests of the school if he gave up his housemastership. Apparently he had been aware of the offences but had done nothing to put an end to them. And what an uproar it caused when it became known that he had to resign! There was a good deal of talk about it all over the school and a lot of distaste expressed. It reached a point when boys felt that words among themselves were doing no good, and they should show their feelings by action and let it be known by the authorities. And this they did! All over the school – on pavements, lamp posts, division rooms, on walls – they started gluing little pieces of paper with slogans, like, 'Save NASH' and 'OUT Trench!' This went on for about four days until each house in the school was sternly lectured by its master and warned about writing these legends, with a threat of serious trouble for any boy found sticking them up. As a result the notes ceased appearing, and many were ripped down.

Mr Nash, whom I personally had known little about, was the subject of a great deal of sympathy from boys, although they admitted he had been weak. But he certainly seemed to be very popular. I heard some time after I had left that he later left Eton voluntarily to take up a headmastership somewhere else. What surprised many people about the whole incident was that it didn't make the headlines of the national press, which usually relished such scandals, and there were lots of scandalmongers in the school who liked informing them for money. Had the matter got into the newspapers, however, then Mr Nash, with all the unfavourable exposure, would most likely not have found his new job as a headmaster.

That was the general state of affairs when I left. Though it might well be thought that our behaviour was very bad, most of us felt that Blackett-Ord was one of the best Captains the house had ever had. He had given everyone freedom and a chance to enjoy life. Certainly this applied to the junior boys who had no longer to spend a quarter of their lives at the school in fear of members of the Library and Debate.

I might just add, in conclusion, that much as I had hoped to,

I never made the Library. This, I was happy to believe, was not because of any unfair discrimination and dislike for me, but because, from the time I was elected into Debate till my departure from Eton, only about six boys had left – all from the Library; and only about five boys had been elected to fill the gap, and all of them had been in Debate longer than I had, so it wasn't yet my turn. All the same, I was quite content to remain in Debate. After Blackett-Ord had become House Captain, an extremely good relationship developed between the Library and Debate. They became much closer, associated more and were hardly aware of the difference in their positions. I, for one, used to be always granted permission by a member of the Library to go inside their sitting-room and play their record player whenever I asked. Before Blackett-Ord became Captain, this would never have been allowed. That was because there had always been little love lost between the Library and Debate. The former was, traditionally, of considerably higher status, and demanded an appropriate degree of deference from the Debate. On the other hand, the reverse did not at all apply, and the Library were accustomed to holding the Debate in little regard.

As well as the goings-on in my house under Blackett-Ord, and the incidents in Mr Nash's house, there were also two more dynamic events which rocketed the school, both of which I was at the centre of. One of them occurred about three weeks before the end of my last term, and it showed how gullible and misinformed most Etonians were about Africa – the Great Witchcraft Scandal. This was all very simple and innocent really. But that didn't stop the whole affair getting into the national papers and creating an enormous amount of fuss. It all began when, towards the beginning of my last year, I took a fancy to practising hypnotism. In all, I attempted to hypnotize boys on thirteen occasions and succeeded on seven of them. The failures were due either to distractions such as slamming doors, yelling and low flying jetliners, or because some of the boys were bad subjects. I had learnt how to hypnotize from my elder brother during one half-term break in my third year, which I spent in his London flat. He had experience in the use of this technique in clinical practice at Guy's Hospital.

The particular incidents which caused the witchcraft scandal was when I hypnotized a boy named Timothy Mason, a dark, fifteen-year-old of middle size. He was a bit deaf in one ear, which gave him the mannerism of always cocking his head on one side when he was listening: a blinking, feeble-looking boy who normally appeared very quiet, and I felt he would prove a rather good subject. So one evening before quiet hour, I went to his room and asked him if he would agree to be hypnotized. Four of his friends were there, and they were all thrilled at the idea, he himself included, and we arranged that they all should come to my room straight after quiet hour.

When they came, I made Mason lie down flat on his back on my bed and the others sit somewhere and not make a sound during the session. I drew the curtains, turned off the light and it began. I proceeded to hypnotize him with a bright pencil torch which I held high above his forehead, moving it slowly from side to side; and as I did so, I spoke in a slow, drowsy tone, clear and unruffled. This was one of the four methods I used and it was successful in sending him into a deep trance after about fifteen minutes. Fortunately none of the noises in the house had been sudden and loud enough to distract his concentration. I told him to stay sleeping and that he could now hear absolutely nothing but my voice. Then I went and turned on the light. And to prove to the four watchers that he really was entranced, I quietly gave one of them a pin from my burry and told him to prick Mason as hard as he pleased, but not before I spoke to Mason again saying that from now on he would be totally insensitive to any touch whatsoever. The boy with the pin then picked up Mason's wrist and really jabbed hard, leaving the pin in for several seconds. Mason did not flutter an eyelid. A tiny drop of blood eased from the wound. And there were wide-eyed mutters of astonishment from the boys.

Then, still talking to Mason, I ordered him to get up slowly. He did so and faced me. Telling him, again, that he would hear nothing but my voice, I instructed him to leave the room, and we went walking down the passage amid the noise of boys screaming and mobbing in other rooms and passages. Mason's eyes were shut, and his arms hung by his sides. He truly looked just like a helpless zombie deprived of his own free will. Then the excitement began. The four boys who had been watching the whole experiment thundered off excitedly, flashing the news about. Within minutes a number of boys had gathered, and next they were shouting with alarm and panic. Frantically they urged me to bring Mason out of his trance at once, said it was dangerous and that I should be stopped from practising hypnosis. The noise got so great that I feared that Mason would probably wake up, despite the fact that I had told him he could hear nothing but my voice. He didn't though: just kept walking along at my side as I directed him. The panic that swept over everybody's face grew worse, and the noise so overwhelming, that I agreed to bring him out of it. A wave of dramatic silence engulfed everybody as I slowly counted from five to one. Mason opened his eyes, rubbed them and looked totally lost and baffled. He reached for his glasses he had recently started wearing, which were stowed away in a pocket. Immediately he was swarmed with questions, and tremendous fuss was made over him. He had no idea what was going on and his mind was totally blank as to what had happened to him. As they told him, they eagerly examined the spot of dried blood where the pin had gone in. More boys gathered, and I quietly looked on, regretting having brought Mason outside my room due to the great noise. The criticism of me soon started again, and I tried unsuccessfully to quieten them with assurances that it was perfectly all right and I knew what I was doing. It so happened, however, that the supper bell went at that moment, and I just walked off disinterestedly, deciding to let them continue arguing. As I went down the stairs, I distinctly heard voices saying, 'Mumbo-jumbo – Onyeama's been doing his mumbo-jumbo again!'

In a day or two, the story had reached many ears outside my house. However, because the Africans had a history of studying the spiritual part of the world and the forces of good and evil – witchcraft and black magic – the boys interpreted it all as witchcraft, and the story was that I had put a spell on Mason and stuck needles into him. I was constantly approached in different parts of the school, especially in Rowland's and in division rooms, and asked if this was true. Irritably, I first of all used to explain to boys what were the correct facts of the matter, until I became sick to death of being asked and denied it point blank without bothering to explain anything.

One half-day about five days later, I was hurrying off to my fourth and final division. It was a fine, but rather cold afternoon, and I recall that there was hardly a soul on the High Street at that moment. I had been held up by the master in my third division, and was left with very little time to get to my next one. I was about to cross on to Keate's Lane at the traffic lights when a short, dark-haired man in his middle thirties, with several cameras slung about his neck, stopped me and asked if I was Mr Onyeama. He introduced himself as being from the *Evening Standard* and said that the Headmaster had made a speech condemning some recent remarks on race by Enoch Powell, and had brought me into it. When I asked him how I was brought in, he appeared rather surprised that I knew nothing about it, saying he thought the Headmaster would have told me. Anyway, he smiled, I would find out in the *Evening Standard* later. He seemed a pleasant and honest fellow, and with no more questions, I consented with pleasure when he asked if he could take my picture. I stood there with my books under my arm, grinning at him as I wondered what the dickens the Headmaster could have said. Then I dashed off to my next division, and was greatly relieved to find that the French master was later than I was.

After a rather tiring game of house football that afternoon, I stopped by the *Evening Standard* placard on my way back, which was just some yards from the boys' entrance of Hodgson House. I was with a group of boys from my house, all of us well decorated with mud. Several other boys wearing the uniform were gathered around, because the placard announced 'Eton Boy Victim of Vicious Campaign!' And that Eton boy was me. I had no money on me to buy a copy, but after one glance, the old cockney newsvendor gave me a free copy, and I stood there in my football kit and brown tweed jacket and read the story. The others from my house crowded round me to have a read. It was one whole column.

Apparently some scandalmongers had been continually phoning the national papers to tell them that I was practising witchcraft at the school and had cast a spell on another boy and stuck needles into him. The Headmaster had completely denied these reports and classified them as malicious and vicious lies to discomfort me, adding that the only basis was a kind of rag. The only mention of Enoch Powell was when the Headmaster spoke about anonymous letters, which had increased after a Powell speech, threatening him for having Africans at the school. The letters had been posted from Manchester and Birmingham. It was his feeling, the Headmaster told the paper, that the accusations against me could have been from Powellites in the school but were more likely to have come from outside. But immediately my feeling was that the calls to the press had been made by scandalmongers in the school with the intention of getting money from the newspaper. I was positive of this, since the question of spell and needles was originally brought up inside the school after I had hypnotized Mason.

As I stood on the pavement and read the report, I was quite shattered; for I could never have dreamed that this was going to turn up. My embarrassment was so great that I must have blushed darker than shoe polish! Nerves and muscles twitched like snakes in my whole body. The embarrassment was intensified when my back underwent a barrage of claps from the group I was with, congratulating me and shouting 'Our Hero!' My embarrassment was unconcealed, and my reaction at the report was a trivial sigh. I somewhat flippantly told the excited boys to ignore the matter, and that it was much ado about nothing. On saying this I made off for my house with the football group, and as we went I told them that it was only the hypnotism affair with Mason, and boys in the school wrongly interpreting it as witchcraft.

Right through till supper the matter was talked about in my house, and caused general excitement. I was irritated by all the questions, flattery and back-claps wherever I went, and just told everybody mildly to pack it up. Lower boys at different intervals swept into my room wanting to be hypnotized, and I just threw them out each time with threats of point marks if they didn't stop coming in.

I had mixed feelings about that publicity: a slight feeling of pride that I was front-page news, but more a feeling of annoyance and embarrassment. Though it was not damaging, it was by no means good publicity. A simple and innocent matter had been falsely magnified out of all proportion by ignorant boys, and made the centre of big, serious controversy – I being the scapegoat. The thought beat hell out of me. I could now understand why the photographer was surprised at my apparent ignorance of the matter: nobody had told me that *this* of all things was going to appear in the press. I just felt happy and relieved that the Headmaster denied it. I felt he dealt with the situation splendidly, and I felt a great sense of respect for him.

Since my picture didn't appear in that edition of the *Evening*

Standard, I expected it to be in one of the papers the next morning. That was indeed the case. All the papers carried the same story, and nearly all the photograph. As soon as I got downstairs on my way to breakfast, I was swarmed by boys. They were delightfully bellowing 'My Hero! You're famous, Dillibe!' and 'Come on, Dillibe, give us a kiss!' The noise was overwhelming as they pushed different papers bearing my grinning face. They were uncontrollable and cornered me from all sides against the wall. I didn't want to, but I was forced to smile, a modest and embarrassed smile – and at the same time trying, with members of the two authorities, to cut down the noise and disperse everybody from there. It took quite some doing, but we eventually succeeded.

In the streets throughout that day I was a staring spectacle for boys, masters, passengers in vehicles, townspeople – everybody. Everywhere else I went it was much the same, and I have to admit that a feeling of importance was mingled with my embarrassment. I was frequently approached by boys who begged to arrange a time for me to hypnotize them. Since the matter had caused so much trouble, I adamantly refused. Even a few masters interrupted their teaching to ask, in a friendly way, what the hell it had all been about. The whole room listened in breathless silence as I nervously explained what had happened, a hollow feeling in my chest. I felt uneasy being watched so intently, and my voice was as jerky as an old phonograph record. Amid the gasps of astonishment when I finished were several ape noises. Everybody passed remarks about hypnotism, and as far as I could make out, none of them liked it.

My housemaster entered my room that night as I was working at my table. He was extremely pleasant and we talked about all the publicity. He was keen to know if I had been aware of any campaign against me anywhere in the school. I assured him that there had not been, and told him what really did happen with Mason and how it all got twisted. He seemed satisfied, and politely told me that so as to prevent any more publicity like this, I should stop practising hypnotism. He then asked if by any chance I knew or had any suspicions as to who had been phoning the press to tell them. I had no idea at all and told him so, and even if I had, I would have been reluctant to say, since it was possible for someone to be expelled for giving information about the school to the press. But all the same, I felt somehow that he didn't believe me. He paused slightly with a look of doubt in his eyes. However, the matter ended there.

The result of all the publicity was that a great influx of letters from people outside the school poured in to me for several days. They all expressed deep sympathy in view of the so-called campaign against me. One of them was from the Member of Parliament for Eton and Slough, Joan Lestor. She expressed her certainty that the vast majority of people in England deplored racialism. I showed it to several boys in my house, a number of whom were Enoch Powell supporters; and most of them, especially the Powellites, scornfully classified it as poppycock!

I did feel deep gratitude for the thoughtfulness of the letter writers, and for one reason or another, I couldn't help feeling a sense of guilt to be so sympathized with. It could possibly have been because I didn't deserve any sympathy at all since there was no campaign. For that reason I didn't think it was worth replying to any of them, and didn't do so.

Despite my housemaster's instruction, I didn't actually stop hypnotism: I had become too intrigued by it. But I didn't practise it in my house any more. There was a boy in another house also with hypnotic powers and I used to go and practise with him. His name was Reginald Oliver, a tall Specialist with wavy brown hair whose father was the Editor of the now defunct *Sphere* magazine. A very reserved and polished fellow, his small, deeply set blue eyes were rather foreboding and magnetic; which, together with his mannerism of mumbling to himself now and again, perfectly suited his great interest in witchcraft and spiritualism. I came to know him by chance during my last term, and we became quite friendly. We practised together on a number of occasions in his room after the witchcraft scandal, but his house was frightfully noisy. Only once was there any success: he was able to hypnotize me. His method was making me sit comfortably in an armchair and from behind looking vertically down into my eyes, speaking in a loud drowsy-toned whisper. This method took him five minutes to send me into a deep trance, in which he gave me a post-hypnotic suggestion of switching off the light. I did so.

On another occasion, using the same method, I had him beautifully going under, his eyes helplessly closing, when suddenly, to my intense fury, a friend of his thundered in. Oliver was jolted awake. The boy stopped dead in his tracks, taken aback at his strange encounter. He apologized when he understood what was happening.

I remained rather annoyed at my failure, and as I was leaving Oliver's house I met a group of boys noisily chatting at the bottom of the stairs. In a fed up manner, I asked them when the most quiet time in this house was, so I could visit Oliver's room and practise hypnosis with him in peace. This practically rendered them speechless. They looked at each other for a reply, and held frowns of surprise and somewhat of suspicion. They couldn't really say. I soon regretted strongly having asked that question, for in no time at all a rumour had started to circulate that I wanted things quiet in Oliver's house so that I could practise homosexuality with him. This rumour reached my ears in different parts of the school, and it always infuriated me when I was asked if it was true.

Yes, homosexuality again! It cropped up once more as a result of the witchcraft publicity. Boys had always thought of me as a homosexual. Now they learn I have been hypnotizing people. So they just simply put two and two together. I was often asked for what purpose I did it. My answer that I just simply liked practising it always seemed too feeble and unsatisfactory, and boys in my house and outside inferred, much to my annoyance, that the point of all my hypnotic experiments was to make people easy prey for sex. I was caused to strongly suspect in view of this that most people believed, and behind my back were saying, the same thing. There was one particular false rumour which added to my suspicion. I heard it one afternoon after a French division. I was walking up Keate's Lane on my way to my house when three good friends in my block caught up with me. To my horror, they mentioned a slanderous rumour they had heard about me and asked if it was true: that I had undressed one of my subjects when he was in a trance, and assaulted him! It was third-hand poppycock with no foundation, and I told them so furiously!

I knew there was no occasion of any nature for such scurrilous gossip. It remained on my mind for a long time afterwards, and as I lay in bed that night, my mind searched feverishly for a possible origin of it. Eventually the explanation rushed upon me with appalling clarity. With painful reminiscence, I focused my mind on the typical questions I was being asked by boys who believed I practised hypnotism for sexual reasons. 'All you do to your subjects when they're in a trance is de-bag them and bugger them, don't you?' or 'Do you queer them up or something?' . . . And undoubtedly they expressed their suspicions to other boys, the matter by and by became distorted, and eventually boiled down that I actually assaulted a subject.

Fortunately, I never heard that particular rumour again. If I had, my worry would have become overwhelming anguish. Because, for several days I was trying vainly to dispel some thoughts that were hammering at my brains: what if some mean scandalmongers who had swallowed the rumours about my sex-hypnotic practices were to start phoning the press again, and more publicity followed as a result? . . . Whatever the consequences, I would, I bitterly acknowledged, be in a pretty hot position. For as a member of Debate, it would be regarded especially bad that I had disobeyed my housemaster and continued practising hypnotism, particularly as he had ordered me to stop for the sake of preventing any more publicity.

As it happened, what would most likely have caused a hair-raising uproar, never arose; but my worry that it might was the cause of my packing up hypnosis. This was a week or two after the witchcraft scandal.

The other event of which I was the centre was when I did a

Black Power salute in public, and that also got into the national papers. But it was just a joke really. It happened, actually, a little over a week before the witchcraft scandal: on the last night of a four-day school performance of *Antony and Cleopatra*, in which I made three brief appearances as a Roman messenger and had only one line to speak. The play was held in the New Theatre, and the audience included members of the staff and the public as well as boys.

However, after I had made all my appearances, I and quite a number of boys were hanging around in one of the changing rooms. We were rather impatiently waiting for the end so that we could make our curtain-call. The boring atmosphere of the untidy room was suddenly charged by excitement when one of the cast rushed in, eyes blazing excitedly. He came up to me and drew everybody's attention by announcing that, despite my tiny part, I should make myself the centre of attraction by doing a Black Power salute at the curtain-call. Just about everybody agreed and urged me to do it, saying it would cause considerable amusement. I was thrilled at the idea, and when I agreed, it produced cheers and back-claps. Only a few thought it would be in bad taste. Pretty well everybody, actually, thought I wouldn't have the guts to do it.

When we all gathered on backstage as the time came, someone brought me a black glove for my right fist. An overwhelming cataclysm of cold nervousness was vibrating my whole body as I waited, and my heart was doing somersaults under my beautiful red toga. This emotion was partly due to the restlessness of everybody around me eager to see if I would really do this daring act, and partly due to my knowledge that I was definitely going to do it. The blood sang in my head when next second, the curtains were opened a few feet. We went out, one at a time from each side of the stage, to meet in the middle, go out through the gap in the curtains and stand there. I was in about the fourth pair, and as soon as I stepped through the curtains, I brought up my arm in the famous salute and kept it there until all the cast had presented themselves, with a broad grin on my face. Amidst the thunderous ovation for our performance were ripples of laughter and several hurrays, which I knew were directed at my gesture.

There was a lot of amusement and discussion about it later in the dressing-room, and I was heartily congratulated by everybody for having had the courage to do it. It was thought that the salute was on the whole received in quite good fun; that since I was grinning, the audience knew that this was obviously a harmless jape. Even the youngish master who produced the play was full of amusement and praises for me.

The incident reached quite a lot of people in the school the following day, and as I might have known, it became exaggerated. The story that circulated was that I had done the salute as a demonstration, and all I could do about it was to correct boys when they questioned me over the matter. But that story, it seemed, had already reached the national papers. Two days after that performance the salute was reported fairly lengthily in the *Daily Express* and briefly in the *Daily Telegraph*. It was only then that I learnt that the Headmaster had been in the audience – sitting in one of the front rows of seats. He was quoted as saying that the salute was pre-arranged, just a light-hearted touch and was all in good fun.

He completely denied that it was meant as a demonstration, which was why it seemed that whoever informed the press must have said it was a demonstration.

The stir that the reports caused was nothing like as great as the witchcraft reports a week or so later. But it did, all the same, produce a lot of gossip. As usual I was engulfed by a feeling of concealed pride and arrogance about it, especially when people wanted to talk to me because I was the centre of news.

I must stress that the publicity which resulted from the Black Power and witchcraft events was, in one very significant way, to my advantage, and for that reason I found it very welcome. I became very much aware of how popular I was now becoming as a result with most people. And, too, how the racial abuse was now getting scanty, and how all my enemies were now becoming friendlier and very keen to talk to me. For nearly four years bitter hostility had existed like a tangible thing between us. Now we could look each other in the eyes and talk amicably like civilized people. And all the changes in everybody was because I had made the headlines. I don't recall ever using violence again after the newspaper reports about the Black Power salute came out, or threatening it.

When I think of the whole situation, I tend to find one thing a bit comical: in all the years I had been at the school, most of the boys didn't want to know me nor have anything to do with me except revile me. But just as I was about to leave they really started to become interested and curious about me.

238

Chapter Eleven
Farewell

A leaving Etonian had nothing much to worry about during his last few weeks except what he was going to do with all the properties belonging to him that had decorated his room over the years – the ottoman, the armchair, the carpet and the bootbox. He could arrange for them to be transferred to his home. But most boys preferred to sell them to one of the two independent furniture shops down the High Street. If his furniture was in reasonable condition, a boy could sell each item for a minor sum, and wouldn't get very much more than £5 for the lot. The furniture would be collected after he had left. That was what I did.

The only events of any significance that I can recall ever occurring during a boy's last few weeks were his attending farewell drinks and a few parties in the night. These were given by people who had influenced his life in the school most – the dame, his housemaster, his Modern tutor and his former Classical tutor. It was not a tradition: it was only done when there were a fair number of boys leaving who were in the same house or had been under the same Modern or Classical tutors. There were four other boys leaving from my house, all members of the Library, and we were also invited to a party with my first housemaster and his wife in their new home.

And so the time had at last come for me to say farewell to Eton College. I was in no doubt whatsoever that most of the boys in my house and divisions would be glad to see the back of me, since they had been saying so for years. But there were, however, a number of boys who said it was a pity I was going. Some of them, I felt, genuinely meant it; others did not – just being courteous. I recall that I was occasionally asked by boys, a few masters and shopkeepers, whether I was sorry to be leaving. I always replied that I was glad to have been at Eton, which was the genuine truth, my reason being that it was good to have been a member of the world's most famous school. But, somewhat regretfully, I always said I was not sorry to be leaving. I only used to give one reason for that: because I was longing for independence and a desire to see more of the world that I had, up until that time, only read about. That was partly the reason, but it was not the real reason. I felt too shy to say truthfully that given a chance, I would not like to live through those four years again. Because, despite the school's impressive privileges and traditions and the numerous enjoyable times that I had there, I had never really been liked or accepted. Above all I hated and had been affected by all the racial abuse more than I'd liked the school's merits – which, therefore, made all the pleasures of the place less enjoyable. And also because I felt so terrible and self-conscious at being constantly bad at work amid boys much younger than I, and my race being believed the cause for it. Those were the real reasons why I was not sorry to be leaving: I just felt altogether out of place.

As I mentioned earlier in the book, one traditional way for leavers to say goodbye to friends and acquaintances was by giving them photographs of themselves. On average, a boy had about eighty photographs taken of him, and the money went on his bill. It wasn't compulsory, however, to have photos taken, and you got the odd boy who couldn't be bothered. I didn't think there was any need really to have more than thirty pictures taken. A dozen of those went to masters, gym-staff and shopkeepers, and the rest to boys. To distribute photos to houses, all the leavers in a house, so long as they were in Debate or Library, congregated in the House Captain's room with their photos, had them all put together by the fags, and arranged in groups of the houses they were destined for. This took place on the last or second to last day of term, and the fags would take them to the houses and leave them on the racks. Photographs for staff were taken to them personally by the leavers.

My last few days did not pass without one major event, in which a lot of serious mischief was involved. A big feast was held on the final night in the room of a member of Debate, and went on till about three in the morning. There were about ten of us in the room, and the feast was a farewell get-together for the leavers. Most of us were still in our uniforms, and only a few were in dressing-gowns and pyjamas. We were seated on the ground, smoking and drinking gin and brandy. The room was full of smoke, and we were talking and joking in normal tones.

After a while two boys, one a member of the Library and the other of Debate, brought up an idea that had apparently been planned some weeks before the term ended: to smash up the Pop-room. This was on the High Street in a building called the Old Christopher, separated from Hodgson House by the drive to my housemaster's. The building was out of bounds to boys, since it was where the boys' maids slept. Pop-room was on the ground floor. Everybody in the feast was restlessly thrilled at the idea of smashing it up, and various methods were lengthily discussed, including blowing it up – how exactly, I was never sure. But it was finally decided to make a mess in there and break all the windows. There was one drawback though: what if there were some Pops inside? . . . It was then agreed that someone should go and look from the Library window, which was on the first floor opposite, and see if the lights were on or off. But there was yet another problem to be answered. Pop-room had heavy curtains, and what if they should by any chance be drawn? Everybody's mind wrestled calmly with that problem. The answer seemed to be that someone should hurl heavy objects from the Library window, try and break the Pop-room windows and see if anyone rushed out. And who would do that? . . . Well, I was a powerful bowler for the Twenty-Two, wasn't I? And so I was elected. A little machine in the back of my head told me not to get involved, and at first was unwilling to do it. But I was urged on by everybody and assured that they would pay for all the damage if we were caught, and so, somewhat reluctantly, I agreed.

The two ringleaders and I went down to the Library, and from there, in the dark, we could see that the curtains were drawn, but not tightly, and there was a light on. But was anyone there? . . . I tried to nurse an inner excitement and agitation as one of them noiselessly opened the bottom half of the window while the other groped his way to the Library sock-cupboard and took out three empty jamjars. Then in a state of mounting tension, I crouched by the open, moonlit window, clouds of vapour coming from my mouth in the cold air, and slung the first jar with every ounce of my strength. There was a stunning crash as it splintered on the wall a few feet from the windows. Quickly I slid down the window and we crouched down out of sight in breathless silence, waiting to hear the reaction. There was none.

'They probably didn't hear it,' whispered the boy in Debate.

'They mightn't even be in there,' replied the other.

'Then why's the fucking light on?'

'Probably forgot to turn it off,' I said.

They wanted to try again. I agreed, and taking my time, tried to be as accurate as possible. But to my annoyance, my second shot was wider, though just as loud. No result. A few seconds I tried again on their request – for the final time. The shot was much the same as the other two, but this time there was a result. We could hear a door loudly squeaking open.

'Don't be seen, Dillibe, for God's sake,' said the Library member.

But I couldn't help peeking. I saw our housemaster in dressing-gown and slippers, coming out of a door near the gate into his own drive-way. 'It's tutor,' I hissed.

The other two sighed helplessly and wondered what the hell to do next.

'I think I'll go and pacify him,' whispered the Library member decidedly. 'You two go back upstairs. I know what I'll say to him.'

We got back to where the others were smoking and drinking and gave the warning. We waited quietly with the lights off, speaking in low tones. It was about five minutes later that the

Library member came back, and we all eagerly asked what had happened.

'I told him that I thought that the Pops were deliberately making a row as an end-of-term joke. We went into Pop-room since the lights were on. There wasn't anybody in there but he's convinced that they must have been responsible.'

There was a good deal of laughter and congratulations all round at this splendid lie. A brilliant piece of work, we felt.

Most of us bade each other farewell and best wishes after all that, then dispersed to our rooms, except two ringleaders, who went to perform their duty in Pop-room. A few boys hung around patiently on the landings waiting for their return. I hadn't quite finished my packing and spent some time doing so. I didn't know when the ringleaders returned from Pop-room, but before I went to bed – sometime around 4 a.m. – I had gone to the room of one of the boys who had waited for them to find out what they eventually did. He told me that Pop-room had been pretty well done over, chairs and other breakables smashed, and so on. I never heard what the reaction was, if any.

The break-up day, 11th December 1968, was grey and depressing – almost like the day I had first joined the school. I overslept in the morning until about eleven, after all the late-night activities. I was awoken by the deafening roar of a jet scraping the rooftops on its way out from London Airport. Apart from that the whole house was very quiet. I knew that everyone was pretty well home by now. I was still very sluggish as I slowly got out of bed and went to wash in the basin. The water was, of course, cold by now; I never heard the boys' maid enter at 7.30 a.m. I changed into my dark suit. I had one important task to do before dashing off – to go and thank my first housemaster for all he had done for me. This had never left my mind since that confrontation I had with him on the last night of his last term.

I was soon outside in the cold but refreshing air briskly walking the half-mile to his house. Some Etonians were lolling around, waiting for parents, taxis or buses, and as usual almost unrecognisable in bell-bottomed trousers, jeans and leather jackets, and even Carnaby Street gear. I spent five minutes with my first housemaster and his wife in their sitting-room, and with deep sincerity expressed my thanks for all his great kindness and help, and I gave him a leaving photo. My conscience was now clear. I was soon on my way back again – this time to collect my baggage and go. I went to the bus stop opposite the School Hall building where a few Etonians were waiting. The bus came after a while and we clambered on for London. I was first going to stay with friends for a week, arranging permanent hostel accommodation from where I would attend my coaching establishment next term. After that week, I would fly off to Holland for Christmas with my family.

I have to admit that as the double-decker Green Line chugged away and the last remnants of Eton slowly disappeared behind me, I really did feel a heavy lump in my throat. I felt the sudden realization of the enormity of what was happening flood over me in a cold wave. I was leaving ETON COLLEGE! There seemed more to the name than met the ear. For a reason I cannot explain, it seemed so unbelievable, so unreal! It was as if I knew I was leaving Heaven for good and didn't care. I was going away from a lot of glory, luxury and comfort into a tough world, full of hardships, where one had to fend for himself – and yet, at the same time, I seemed quite content with it that way. Only the interruption of the conductor asking for my fare jolted me from my thinking. But I soon returned to it again. I was sitting alone in my seat upstairs, and once again, almost like four years before, I became almost hypnotized in my thoughts. I was unaware of the world outside and my fellow creatures sitting around me. Whatever happened, I knew, I was always going to be proud of Eton. I knew it was going to forever influence my life, in some way, and I would win respect from people because I had been there. Even if I was rather stupid, it had taught me a lot academically. And its colour prejudice, also, taught me one thing about myself and my people: that I am BLACK, and this is a world in which the black man has to suffer. I am left with one candid belief about the black man as a result of having lived with him for the last two years since I left Eton: that God especially created him to suffer, and he will always suffer.

BLACK BRITAIN: WRITING BACK

MINTY ALLEY
C. L. R. JAMES

Selected by Booker Prize-winning author
Bernardine Evaristo, this series rediscovers
and celebrates pioneering books depicting
Black Britain that remap the nation.

It is the 1920s in the Trinidadian capital, and Haynes's world has
been upended. His mother has passed away, and his carefully
mapped-out future of gleaming opportunity has disappeared with
her.

Unable to afford his former life, he finds himself moving into
Minty Alley – a bustling barrack yard teeming with life and a
spectacular cast of characters. In this sliver of West Indian
working-class society, outrageous love affairs and passionate
arguments are a daily fixture, and Haynes begins to slip from
curious observer to the heart of the action.

Minty Alley is a gloriously observed portrayal of class, community
and the ways in which we are all inherently connected. An undis-
puted modern classic, this is an exceptional story told by one of the
twentieth century's greatest Caribbean thinkers.

BLACK BRITAIN: WRITING BACK

BERNARD AND THE CLOTH MONKEY
JUDITH BRYAN

Selected by Booker Prize-winning author
Bernardine Evaristo, this series rediscovers
and celebrates pioneering books depicting
Black Britain that remap the nation.

When Anita finally returns to London after a long absence,
everything has changed.

Her father is dead, her mother has disappeared and she and her
sister Beth are alone together for the first time in years.

They share a house. They share a family. They share a past.

Tentatively, they reach out to each other for connection, but the
house echoes with words unspoken. Can they confront the pain of
the past together?

Dazzling and heartbreaking, *Bernard and the Cloth Monkey* is
a shattering portrait of family, a rebellion against silence and a
testament to the human capacity for survival.

BLACK BRITAIN: WRITING BACK

WITHOUT PREJUDICE
NICOLA WILLIAMS

Selected by Booker Prize-winning author
Bernardine Evaristo, this series rediscovers
and celebrates pioneering books depicting
Black Britain that remap the nation.

Lee Mitchell is a thirty-year-old barrister from a working-class
Caribbean background: in the cut-throat environment of the
courtroom, everything is stacked against her.

After she takes on the high-profile case of notorious millionaire
playboy Clive Omartian – arrested along with his father and step-
brother for eye-wateringly exorbitant fraud – the line between her
personal and professional life becomes dangerously blurred.

Spiralling further into Clive's trail of debauchery and corruption,
she finds herself in alarmingly deep waters.

Can she survive her case, let alone win it?

BLACK BRITAIN: WRITING BACK

THE DANCING FACE
MIKE PHILLIPS

Selected by Booker Prize-winning author
Bernardine Evaristo, this series rediscovers
and celebrates pioneering books depicting
Black Britain that remap the nation.

University lecturer Gus knows that stealing the priceless Benin
mask, The Dancing Face, from a museum at the heart of the British
establishment will gain an avalanche of attention.

But such risky theft will also inevitably capture the attention of
characters with more money, more power and fewer morals.

Naively entangling his loved ones in his increasingly dangerous
pursuit of righteous reparation, is Gus prepared for what it will cost
him?

BLACK BRITAIN: WRITING BACK

THE FAT LADY SINGS

JACQUELINE ROY

Selected by Booker Prize-winning author
Bernardine Evaristo, this series rediscovers
and celebrates pioneering books depicting
Black Britain that remap the nation.

'That is the glory of being a mental patient, nothing is impossible.'

It is the 1990s, and Gloria is living in a London psychiatric ward.
She is unapologetically loud, audacious and eternally on the
brink of bursting into song. After several months of uninterrupt-
ed routine, she is joined by another young Black woman – Merle –
who is full of silences and fear.

Unable to confide in their doctors, they agree to journal their pasts.
Whispered into tape recorders and scrawled ferociously at night,
the remarkable stories of their lives are revealed.

In this tender, deeply moving depiction of mental health, Roy
creates a striking portrait of two women finding strength in their
shared vulnerability, as they navigate a system that fails to protect
them.

Life-affirming and fearlessly hopeful, this is an unforgettable story.

BLACK BRITAIN: WRITING BACK

INCOMPARABLE WORLD
S. I. MARTIN

Selected by Booker Prize-winning author Bernardine Evaristo, this series rediscovers and celebrates pioneering books depicting Black Britain that remap the nation.

In the years just after the American Revolution, London was the unlikely refuge for thousands of Black Americans who fought for liberty on the side of the British.

Buckram, Georgie and William have earned their freedom and escaped their American oppressors, but on the streets of London, poverty awaits with equal cruelty.

Ruthless, chaotic and endlessly evolving, London forces them into a life of crime, and a life on the margins. Their only hope for a better future is to concoct a scheme so daring it will be a miracle if it pays off.

Pulsating with energy and vivid detail, *Incomparable World* boldly uncovers a long-buried narrative of Black Britain.

BLACK BRITAIN: WRITING BACK

BRITONS THROUGH NEGRO SPECTACLES
A. B. C. MERRIMAN-LABOR

**Selected by Booker Prize-winning author
Bernardine Evaristo, this series rediscovers
and celebrates pioneering books depicting
Black Britain that remap the nation.**

A riotous, witty travelogue documenting the author's experiences
in Britain in the early 1900s, from an African perspective.

'*We shall therefore confine our walk to Central London where
people meet on business during the day, and to West London
where they meet for pleasure at night. If you will walk about the
first City in the British Empire arm in arm with Merriman-Labor,
you are sure to see Britons in* merriment *and at* labour, *by night
and by day . . .*'

In *Britons Through Negro Spectacles* Merriman-Labor takes us on
a joyous, intoxicating tour of London at the turn of the twentieth
century.

Slyly subverting the colonial gaze usually placed on Africa, he
introduces us to the citizens, culture and customs of Britain with a
mischievous glint in his eye.

This incredible work of social commentary provides unique
insights into the intersection between Empire, race and community
at this important moment in history.

'A buried treasure of a book . . . the author was a century
ahead of his time'

Bernardine Evaristo

BLACK BRITAIN: WRITING BACK

SEQUINS FOR A RAGGED HEM
AMRYL JOHNSON

**Selected by Booker Prize-winning author
Bernardine Evaristo, this series rediscovers
and celebrates pioneering books depicting
Black Britain that remap the nation.**

A beautifully atmospheric memoir and travelogue from poet Amryl
Johnson depicting her journey from the UK to Trinidad in the
1980s.

*'Memories demanded that I complete this book. If what I
experienced was, in fact, a haunting, I believe I have now laid these
ghosts to rest in a style which I hope will satisfy even the most
determined ones.'*

Amryl Johnson came to England from Trinidad when she was
eleven. As an adult in 1983, ready for a homecoming, she embarks
on a journey through the Caribbean searching for home, searching
for herself.

Landing in Trinidad as carnival begins, she instantly surrenders to
the collective, pulsating rhythm of the crowd, euphoric in her total
freedom. This elation is shattered when she finds the house where
she was born has been destroyed. She cannot – nor wants to –
escape from the inheritance of colonialism.

Her bittersweet welcome sets the tone for her intoxicating explora-
tion of these distinct islands. In evocative, lyrical prose, *Sequins for
a Ragged Hem* is an astonishingly unique memoir, interrogating the
way our past and present selves live alongside each other.

BLACK BRITAIN: WRITING BACK

MY FATHERS' DAUGHTER
HANNAH-AZIEB POOL

Selected by Booker Prize-winning author Bernardine Evaristo, this series rediscovers and celebrates pioneering books depicting Black Britain that remap the nation.

'When I stepped off the plane in Asmara, I had no idea what lay ahead, or how those events would change me . . .'

In her twenties, Hannah-Azieb Pool is given a letter that unravels everything she knows about her life. She knew she was adopted from an orphanage in Eritrea, and as her adoptive family brought her to the UK, they believed she did not have any surviving relatives.

When she discovers the truth in a letter from her brother – that her birth father is alive and her Eritrean family are desperate to meet her – she is faced with a critical choice.

Should she go?

In this intimate memoir, she takes us with her on an extraordinary journey of self-discovery, as she travels to Eritrea to uncover her own story. With radiant warmth, courage and wisdom, Hannah-Azieb disentangles the charged concepts of identity, family and home. Featuring a new introduction from Bernardine Evaristo and an updated afterword from the author, this is a timeless, essential read.

'What a story. So vivid, honest and moving'

Andrea Levy

WWW.PENGUIN.CO.UK

BLACK BRITAIN: WRITING BACK

GROWING OUT
BARBARA BLAKE HANNAH

Selected by Booker Prize-winning author Bernardine Evaristo, this series rediscovers and celebrates pioneering books depicting Black Britain that remap the nation.

A beautiful memoir written by the first Black female TV journalist about her experience migrating from the Caribbean to the UK, and the beauty and struggle of being a woman during that period.

Travelling over from Jamaica as a teenager, Barbara's journey is remarkable. She finds her footing in TV, and blossoms. Covering incredible celebrity stories, travelling around the world and rubbing shoulders with the likes of Germaine Greer and Michael Caine, her life sparkles. But with the responsibility of being the first Black woman reporting on TV comes an enormous amount of pressure, and a flood of hateful letters and complaints from viewers that eventually costs her the job.

In the aftermath of this fallout, she goes through a period of self-discovery that allows her to carve out a new space for herself first in the UK and then back home in Jamaica – one that allows her to embrace and celebrate her Black identity, rather than feeling suffocated in her attempts to emulate whiteness and conform to the culture around her.

Growing Out provides a dazzling, revelatory depiction of race and womanhood in the 1960s from an entirely unique perspective.

'A gorgeously exuberant account'

Bernardine Evaristo